BEDOUIN COMMAND

With the Arab Legion 1953–1956

Lt.-Col. Peter Young
D.S.O., M.C. and two Bars

BEDOUIN COMMAND

Published by Sapere Books.

24 Trafalgar Road, Ilkley, LS29 8HH

United Kingdom

saperebooks.com

ISBN: 978-1-80055-999-8.

TABLE OF CONTENTS

FOREWORD
by Lt.-Gen. Sir John Glubb,
K.C.B., C.M.G., D.S.O., O.B.E., M.G.

Lt.-Colonel Young has given us a regimental soldier's book. In reading it, the first impression the British officer might receive is that soldiering is always the same.

Substitute Smith, Jones and Robinson for Muhammad, Saud, or Salama, and you have the daily chronicles of a British battalion.

It is all the same — and yet is so entirely different. Internally the Arab Legion was an army like any other army, but latterly, unlike the British Army, it was exposed to immensely strong pressures from outside, and the pressures were passionate, emotional and in many cases the result of genuine grievances. Particularly was this the case as regards the Palestine problem. Nothing, in my opinion, can justify the tragic muddle of which the British Government was guilty in Palestine.

In the opinion of most of the Arabs of Palestine, Britain was the principal cause of the tragedy which resulted in the exile of nearly a million of their number from their homes, and their continued existence for eight years as homeless refugees. Believing Britain to be the cause of their ruin, it was not altogether surprising that the Palestine Arabs were mistrustful of the Arab Legion under its British commanders, as a defence against Israel.

And yet they were wrong. Most of the British officers of the Arab Legion were extremely devoted to their troops, completely loyal to their duty to Jordan and intensely proud of the high military standards attained. A few of us had devoted our lives to the service of the Arabs and had been bitterly opposed to British policy in Palestine.

Colonel Young, at the beginning of his book, plunges straight into the details of his regimental duties. Perhaps it may assist the reader if I can introduce him to the subject from a wider point of view.

At the end of the First World War, Palestine, the strip of country between the Jordan river and the Mediterranean, was placed by the League of Nations under a British Mandate. The territory east of the Jordan and extending out into the desert of Northern Arabia was made into a separate principality under the Amir Abdulla. A small force was raised to keep order in this new state of Trans-Jordan, and it was called the Arab Legion. It was partly military and partly police.

In 1926 the British Government also raised a force in Palestine and Trans-Jordan, known as the Trans-Jordan Frontier Force. This force was purely military and was an Imperial unit, with British officers down to the level of squadron commanders. The Arab Legion, on the contrary, was entirely under the orders of the Trans-Jordan Government, and contained only two British officers. These officers were servants of the Trans-Jordan Government.

In 1940 the Arab Legion, which for fourteen years had been limited to a police role, once more formed military units, and these units fought side by side with the British Army throughout the war. During the Second World War the strength of the Arab Legion increased from 1,400 in 1939 to 16,000 in 1945. It consisted of two wings, a military and a police wing. It thus constituted the army and the police force of the State of Trans-Jordan. It was never a British force or part of the British Army, though Britain paid a grant-in-aid to

Trans-Jordan to support it. Its status vis-à-vis the British Army was that of an Allied Army.

At the end of the Second World War the economy axe fell heavily and the authorized establishment for 1948 was down to 6,000. But in May 1948 the British Mandate in Palestine came to an end, and the Arab Legion became involved in heavy fighting with the troops of the new State of Israel. Incidentally, the Arab Legion did not invade Israel, as is often stated. The Arab Legion never reached the borders of Israel as laid down by the United Nations. It everywhere encountered the Israeli forces in territory allotted to the Arabs, which the Israelis had penetrated before the Arab Legion arrived on the scene.

The Arab Legion alone, of all the Arab Armies, enhanced its reputation in the fighting with the Jews. If the Arabs as a whole were defeated, this did not apply to the Arab Legion, which was everywhere successful. That portion of Palestine which was saved for the Arabs was defended solely by the Arab Legion and the Iraqi Army. Nothing could be further from the truth than to say that the Egyptian and Syrian armies were the heroes, and that the Arab Legion and Iraqi Army had betrayed the cause.

In the eight years from 1948 to 1956 the strength of the Arab Legion was built up from 6,000 to 27,000, including four thousand police. Behind the Arab Legion, the regular Army, a National Guard was created on the lines of the Territorial Army. By 1956 the National Guard could put about 30,000 men in the field. To raise a force of 6,000 to nearly 60,000, or tenfold, in the course of eight years, was a military feat of some magnitude. If we look back to 1940, we find that the Arab Legion in fifteen years increased from 1,400 to nearly 60,000, or more than forty-fold. Now fifteen years is enough in which to produce N.C.O.s and junior officers, but it is not enough to produce senior officers.

Thus the Arab Legion in 1956 was in the peculiar situation of consisting of 27,000 regulars and 30,000 territorials, although the most senior Jordanian officer with modern training was only thirty-six years old. The great majority were in their early twenties. In Jordan, we were fully aware that the Jordanians wanted naturally enough to assume command of their own army, but we were faced with this problem of the rapid expansion which had taken place and the inexperience of the officer cadre. We discussed this very fully and frankly with the Jordanian officers, and many-phased plans for the hand-over from British to Arab Command were discussed. The King was aware of all this, and expressed his approval.

But while the army was thus endeavouring to decide its own future on the basis of military efficiency, politics and emotional nationalism stepped in. Arab nationalism is a typical upsurge of emotion in the modern world. Britain herself first sponsored it in World War One and on many subsequent occasions. But various factors, particularly the rise of Israel, had confused the original issue of British support for Arab aspirations. Egypt, who herself has ambitions to be leader of the Arabs, was anxious to sever the link between them and Britain, in order that she should become the Sovereign of an Arab Empire. Thus hatred of Israel (of whom Britain was accused of being the friend) and the rising ambitions of Egypt combined to create a coldness — even a hostility — between Britain and Arab nationalism.

Trans-Jordan — now renamed Jordan — had for thirty-five years been Britain's most loyal ally in the Arab world. Such a voluntary friendly association provided an almost unanswerable reply to Egypt's thesis that to get rid of the

British was the first essential for all Arab countries. The Egyptians therefore set themselves to upset the hitherto happy relations between Jordan and Britain.

King Husain had himself been touched by the emotional enthusiasm of nationalism. Youth all over the world is filled by ideals for which it longs to fight. It is only in middle life that we discover that these questions are not so simple as they appear, and that the world is not really sharply divided into heroes and villains. I told the King that I was his servant and not that of the British Government, and that if he wished it, I would resign. But it is difficult for a man past middle-age to enjoy the full confidence of a young man of twenty. He had other advisers nearer his own age.

And so the end of my service came in a manner which I regretted. The same result could have been achieved so easily without disturbance or friction. And with the end of the Arab Legion, for that title has now been abolished and replaced by that of the Jordan Arab Army, the uniforms, the organization, everything has been changed.

This was the background against which Lieut.-Col. Young completed his service with the Arab Legion.

Westwood St. Dunstan,
Mayfield, Sussex.

CHAPTER I: JORDAN

In November 1951 I was posted to G.H.Q. Middle East Land Forces, and served for the next sixteen months as a GSO 2 in the G. Training and Infantry Branch of that Headquarters. During that period a large-scale signals exercise, Exercise Hatta, was held in Jordan in co-operation with the Arab Legion. This exercise was organized by G. Training, and I was one of the officers sent to Amman beforehand to arrange the details. Two officers of my own Regiment, Pincher Martin and Morris Brightman, were serving in the Legion, and the latter, who worked in Qiada (Headquarters) invited me to stay.

From what I saw of the country and the Legion it soon became clear to me that it would be a mistake to remain in Fayid. The whole atmosphere here was quite different to the Canal Zone. The reputation of the Legion stood very high in G.H.Q., and indeed the keenness and efficiency of the Arab soldiers were very evident. One could tell from their saluting and their turnout that they were proud to be soldiers: here every man was a volunteer. Before Exercise Hatta ended I was convinced that this would be a wonderful army to serve with, but it was not easy to get in — not merely a matter of offering one's services — for of the sixty British officers not more than a dozen were infantrymen, and of these only four commanded battalions. During Hatta I had got to know one of them, James Watson, who told me that he himself was leaving in six months' time. General Cooke, the commander of the 1st Division, was a friend of my G. III, Bob Ambrose, who advised me to write and say that I would like to join the Legion. The General's reply was encouraging, and in February

1953 I was told that I had been selected to succeed James Watson.

I soon had a letter from James in answer to various questions:

"Naturally I have to tell you that you are taking over the best Regiment in the Legion — the 9th. *I* founded it three years ago...

"There is only one British person in the Regt. (ME!)... I have copies of my remarks on the officers' confidential reports last month and will give you all the 'real' information verbally...

"You also wanted to know about servants. All of mine are in the Regiment and will naturally become yours. The Cook (Hassan), a Sudani, is very willing and produces good plain food at a reasonable price. The 'Butler', also a Sudani (Omer), is mental and I recommend that he is sent home... I will keep an eye open for one for you. The difficulty is that Sudanis work well together, but if you mix them with, say, a Palestini, there is trouble.

"Do you remember my dog — a small Alsatian bitch (Tigla) with a charming nature? Would you like to take her on? There are plenty of people here who would like her, but as you will have at least three years to do I'd sooner you had her.

"I forgot three of the servants. The Batman, a very religious Bedouin (Haj Ibrahim), is first class. He can't read or write but looks after master well. In addition to the normal batman's duties he is good in the house, at cleaning up and making beds.

"Two drivers for the Humber (Awwad Ahmed) and Land-Rover (Mahmoud), are very good and, in many years of driving, have never had an accident. NONE of the servants speak English....

"My tour finishes on 14 April: a new Brig., Green of the Middlesex, takes over from John McCully in June."

I arrived at Mafraq on 19th March, and once more went to live with the Brightmans.

The Hashemite Kingdom of the Jordan, lying East and West of the great river from which it takes its name, is split in two by the deep rift of the Jordan valley. To the East the former British Mandate of Transjordan became in 1946 an independent sovereign state under King Abdulla. To the West that part of Palestine which was not overrun by the Israelis in 1948 was annexed and now forms part of the Hashemite Kingdom.

On either side of the Jordan valley mountains rise sharply to about 2,500 feet above sea level. Jericho is 700 feet below the Mediterranean, while Jerusalem, only fifteen miles to the West, is 2,600 feet above that level. To the East the plateau of Transjordan is some 3,500 feet higher than Jericho. The Jordan valley is a great gulf fixed between the two parts of the Hashemite Kingdom.[1]

Palestine, a country somewhat larger than Wales, is now divided between Jordan, Egypt and Israel. Egypt holds little but Gaza, and Jordan, generally speaking, holds the Judaean hills. When the Israelis carved their state out of Palestine they secured the district round Nazareth, which was inhabited almost entirely by Arabs; the fertile coastal plain; and the barren Negeb. In due course they established their capital in the western suburbs of Jerusalem.

In 1948, when Great Britain surrendered her Mandate[2] for Palestine, severe fighting broke out between Arabs and Jews:

----

[1] The terms East Bank and West Bank are now widely used to describe the provinces commonly called Transjordan and Palestine in former times.

[2] In 1918 the Turks were driven out of Palestine, and the country came under a British Military Government. From 1923 Great Britain ruled Palestine under a Mandate from the League of Nations, which

many people in England seem to believe that as a result the Jews conquered Palestine, which then became Israel. This is far from being the truth. In 1948 large tracts of Palestine were inhabited solely by Arabs, and the armies of the Arab League contrived to defend a considerable part of that territory: Jenin, Nablus, Tulkarm, Qalqilya, Ramallah, the Old City of Jerusalem, Bethlehem, Hebron and Jericho are all in Jordan.

The Israelis hold Nazareth, Beisan, Afule, Haifa, Jaffa and Tel-Aviv, part of Jerusalem and Beersheba.

In biblical terms Gilead, Ammon, Moab and Edom go to make up the Transjordan part of the Hashemite Kingdom, while the Palestinian part consists of Samaria and much of Judah. Only Galilee, the Plain of Sharon, the Philistine Plain and the Negeb are in Israel.

The chief towns of Transjordan are Amman, the capital, which has been growing rapidly since 1948; Zerqa, the Aldershot of the Arab Legion; Salt, Irbid, Ma'an, Mafraq, Madaba, Kerak and Aqaba — the only port.

The climate is pleasant and temperate, much the same as Sicily or Southern Italy. The Jordan valley is intensely hot and enervating in the summer months, but mild and sunny in the winter. Zerqa is a little too hot in the middle of July, but Jerusalem is delightful. Between the end of November and the end of March there is sometimes a rainfall equal to that of an English year. Then in the spring the country is beautiful with wild flowers: cyclamen, anemones, jonquils, iris, lupins, white and yellow daisies, to name but a few, and with multitudes of almond and apricot trees in full blossom; then even the low foothills on the edge of the Syrian Desert have a delicate mantle of green. The rain belt extends roughly to the Hejaz Railway; the desert lies beyond. The climate of places in Jordan

---

she surrendered in 1948.

depends chiefly upon their altitude, but the winds play their part. The west winds bring rain; the north-west breezes are pleasantly cool; the east wind is a curse — hot, dusty and violent — but it does not come too often.

The population of Jordan is estimated to be a million and a half. Of these about one-third are Palestinian refugees. Perhaps one-tenth of the total are nomadic and semi-nomadic bedouin, and the remainder are the indigenous inhabitants of Transjordan and that part of Palestine that remains in Arab hands.

I had gone to Egypt after the abrogation of the Treaty in 1951, and had therefore lived for the last sixteen months where the inhabitants were anxious to show their masters how anti-British they were. When I first went to Jordan I naturally wondered what the political climate there might be, for it can hardly be thought pleasant to soldier with people who hate your guts.

The British Government was spending about nine million pounds a year on the Arab Legion. Officers in G.H.Q. with whom I discussed the matter seemed to believe that in the event of a major war it would take its place alongside a British division in a Corps that would be organized in the Middle East. Before Exercise Hatta ended it had been borne in upon me that this was not the idea of the Arab officers. Their first concern was with Palestine; to them the enemy was Israel.

If the Legion had distinguished itself in the fighting in 1948, the Arabs as a whole had not. The resulting partition of Palestine had been a catastrophe for which Great Britain and the United States of America were chiefly blamed; the latter for her support of Israel. Grievances against Great Britain dated back to the Palestine Mandate.

Any anti-British feeling among the Arabs of Jordan has its roots in the Palestine Problem. No question, military or political, compares with it in their mind in either interest or importance. It is, I think, true to say that with the exception of the bedouin, the people are extremely politically minded. Far more so than the people in the small towns and villages of England. The discussion of politics is not perhaps their only spare-time entertainment, but it ranks high, and a never-failing topic of discussion and conversation, in every mess and coffeeshop, is the Palestine Problem. In so far as Great Britain is concerned the grievances commonly put forward by the Arabs go back not to the Palestine Rebellion of 1936-39 but to 1921. In that year there were serious disturbances, mostly in Jaffa, in which more than fifty people were killed and over one hundred and fifty injured. A Commission of Inquiry, whose members were Sir Thomas Haycraft, Chief Justice of Palestine, Mr. H. C. Luke, Assistant Governor of Jerusalem, and Mr. J. B. Stubbs of the Legal Department concluded that the principal grievances of the Arabs, upon whose individual merits or demerits they did not pronounce, were that Great Britain, when she took over the administration of Palestine, was led by the Zionists to adopt a policy mainly directed towards the establishment of a National Home for the Jews, and not to the equal benefit of all Palestinians. The Arabs thought that the Government of Palestine had, as its official advisory body, a Zionist Commission, bound by its ideals and its conception of its role to regard Jewish interests before all others, and that there was an undue proportion of Jews in the Government service. In addition they already complained that it was a part of the programme of the Zionists to flood Palestine with Jewish people, who would eventually obtain the upper hand over the rest of the population.

These grievances had been listed in 1921. If this was the feeling of the Arabs at that time, how much more bitter they must feel in 1953, when most of their gloomy forebodings had been fulfilled.

This report was submitted to the High Commissioner, Herbert Samuel, who forwarded it to the Secretary of State for the Colonies, Winston S. Churchill. For anyone who wishes to understand something of the political outlook of the Arab, particularly the Palestinian Arab, the Reports of this Commission are the best shilling's-worth that ever came out of H.M. Stationery Office. Unfortunately the document is long since out of print, and I should never have known of it had its secretary not been a Mr. E. Bryant, alias Major E. Bryant, M.B.E., D.C.M., better known as "Abu George", who was my next-door neighbour in Zerqa Camp.

It may be said that the grievances, real and imagined, of the Palestine Arabs do not affect those of Transjordan, but two-thirds of the population of the Hashemite Kingdom are now Palestinians, half them being refugees. Of these latter multitudes have been living for the last eight years in the towns of Transjordan. They have had plenty of time to drop the poison of their discontent in the ears of their politically-minded brethren.

But this is background stuff. In 1953 these rankling discontents were not obvious to a British officer, and certainly not to one serving in a bedouin regiment. The Young Officers' Movement had probably been formed after the murder of King Abdulla in 1951. I did not even hear of it until 1954, when John Constant, who had commanded the Sappers, and therefore had more contact with the non-bedouin officers, told me of it. Moreover, although the Arabs continually discussed politics among themselves they seldom broached the subject with the British officers, and in 9 Regiment few of the officers bothered themselves with such things; and in addition, of the Palestinians in the Jeish (army), very few were actually refugees.

On 30th March I went to Mafraq to see my wife off to England. The senior Arab officer, Ahmed Sudqi Pasha el Jundi, was flying on the same plane, and Qaimakam Muhamad Ma'ayta, O.C. Ajlun District, was at the airport to say goodbye to him. Muhamad Ma'ayta, a slim dark smart-looking officer is now the commander of the Arab Legion Royal Artillery. He launched off in excellent English and, with disarming frankness, told me that the Pasha, wanting someone strong for Ajlun District, had offered him the job.

"As you wish," he had modestly replied.

On the way home I had a frustrating conversation with Awwad, the Humber driver, who was trying to point out and describe to me the castle of Hallabat, which lies to the East of the Mafraq-Zerqa road. My Arabic was not up to this.

The next few days I spent on the West Bank staying with Miles Pulford, the commander of 1 Regiment, whom I had met during Exercise Hatta. It was usual for British officers on joining the Legion to do a four-day tour to get an idea of the job and the country. Miles was living in a tent at Jeeb, the Gibeon of the Old Testament, and his regiment was responsible for an enormous area, stretching from Qalqilya in the North to Jerusalem. In those days the Arab Legion kept only one brigade in Palestine. We visited Nigel Bromage, who was then in command of 2 Regiment, at Kufr Itsion. Bromage was a contract officer and had won a Gallantry Medal in the 1948 fighting.

In the evening we went and called on Brigadier "Teal" Ashton at his Brigade H.Q. in Ramallah. He gave us arak to drink, rather like pernod or ouzo, and showed us air photographs of some of the frontier villages. Ashton had been a long time in the Legion, wore a beard, and, like Bromage, spoke fluent Arabic. When in 1948 the British officers were withdrawn by order of our Government, he had somehow contrived to remain at the front. He described conditions on the border, and I remember his telling me how the Israelis had shot up a flock of sheep near the frontier, leaving the wounded shepherd boys to die in the sunshine.

Another day we drove down into the Latrun salient and visited the Templar fortress, Le Toron des Chevaliers, where Richard Coeur de Lion had spent the winter of 1191. Some of the old chambers had been cleared of rubble and made inhabitable through the exertions of Brigadier Ashton, and the place was now garrisoned by the bedouin of 1 Regiment.

We also visited Qalqilya, where the garrison was ensconced in the old Palestine Police Fort. Qalqilya village, on the Tulkarm plain, is in a salient formed by the truce-line laid down at Rhodes in 1949. Nearly all the orange groves belonging to the village now lie in Israel. The people were left only 2,600 of their 7,000 acres, to support a population of 7,020.

When I had been a few days in Amman I was introduced to General Glubb, the Chief of the General Staff of the Arab Legion. The General, who was usually referred to as "the Pasha" was seldom in his office more than three days a week, as he liked to tour around and see things for himself, but he made a point of interviewing all new British officers. He asked me several questions about my previous service, and whether I spoke Arabic. He talked rather slowly and quietly, giving an appearance of benevolence and calm. Although his hair was white, his face did not look old. His clear complexion and twinkling blue eyes gave him rather a youthful expression, despite the marks of a severe wound in the chin. If you looked at him from the side instead of the front, you saw another person, for he had a nose which might have adorned the visage of a Norman baron, and which, when his face was in repose, gave him an air of almost ruthless determination. Such was my impression.

At the conclusion of our interview, during which I never had that uncomfortable feeling that I was being weighed-up, he asked me whether there was anything that could be done to make me comfortable. I said that I hoped there was no difficulty about my taking over James Watson's quarters and at once he picked up one of a battery of telephones and spoke to Colonel Saville, the Quartermaster-General. Half a minute's conversation and the matter was settled. As simple as that.

During the next three years, and particularly while we were in Jerusalem, I was to meet the Pasha many times, when he visited the Regiment or toured the frontier, but it is still extremely difficult for me to describe him. It is almost too easy to say that he was really many different people, but perhaps that does explain it, for he was engineer officer, arabist, policeman, tribal judge, author, minister, and general, not one after the other, but simultaneously. His experience, command of Arabic, immense industry and his mastery of detail so deeply impressed the Jordanians that it gave him great power, for everybody of any importance, both in the Legion and outside it, thought that the Pasha knew all about him, both good and evil. And he probably did.

CHAPTER II: BEDOUIN REGIMENT

9 Regiment, except for No. 4 Company, was raised in 1950 by Lt.-Col. A. J. A. Watson of the Queen's Regiment, an officer who had served many years in the Sudan Defence Force. The cadre of officers, non-commissioned officers and men was drawn from 1 and 7 Regiments, but chiefly from the former, which had also been commanded by Watson. 7 Regiment was reputed to have emptied its prison, when invited to send men to 9, and few of them remained by 1953. No. 4 Company was not raised until 1952.

The second-in-command, who had been adjutant to my predecessor, was Rais Salameh Etayek. He was supposed to be a bedouin from the Shammar, and he certainly came from the South. He was one of the few had married a non-bedouin wife. He was short and stout and limped somewhat from an old wound. In 1948 his company had successfully stormed Radar and an Israeli bullet had broken his leg above the ankle. He had refused to be evacuated until all his wounded had been cared for, and had been decorated with the Gallantry Medal. Later he received the Istiqlal (Class IV) for his services in helping to form and build up 9 Regiment, and the Cedar of Lebanon for a rather indifferent Guard of Honour that he commanded in June 1953, when the Lebanese Prime Minister visited Jordan. I was assured that, despite his unimpressive appearance, I had a first-class second-in-command in Salameh. The trouble about an efficient second-in-command is that he very often thinks he can command the regiment a good deal better than the C.O.

The Regiment was organized like a battalion in the British army, except that it possessed sufficient vehicles to move in its own transport; to that extent it was like a lorried infantry battalion. Regiments on the East Bank had to be ready at any time to move to Palestine in case of aggression by the Israelis, and the delay involved in waiting for troop-carrying vehicles was not acceptable.

In Support Company there were 3-inch mortar, Vickers machine-gun, and anti-tank platoons; the latter originally had 6-pounders, but they were replaced by 17-pounders in 1954. A pioneer platoon was added early in the same year. The rifle companies, as in the British army, each had three platoons of three sections, the bren light machine-gun being the main armament.

In the foot regiments of Charles I's army one-third of the private soldiers were pikemen and two-thirds musketeers. Clearly a most inconvenient arrangement. In Marlborough's day the pikemen disappeared, and thereafter the regimental officer had only to teach his men one weapon: the musket. This happy state endured down to the Great War. Then machineguns, mortars, grenades and anti-tank rifles crept in, to be followed in the Second World War by sub-machine-guns, and 6- or 17-pounder anti-tank guns. The last state is worse than the first, and an infantry regiment now has a variety of arms unrivalled in the feudal levies of mediaeval times.

In 9 Regiment we had brens, stens, rifles, sniper rifles, pistols, Vickers machine-guns, 3-inch mortars, 2-inch mortars, 6-pounders, not to mention a variety of grenades, including the Belgian Energa anti-tank grenade. Another complication was that the ranges were marked on the backsight of the rifles in English, while the men, if they could read at all, read Arabic. Long hours were spent teaching them the English figures. An infantry section of nine men would have two different types of ammunition: .303 for the bren and the riflemen, and 9 mm. for the sten.

Though the organization and armament of the Regiment was practically that of a British battalion, the similarity ended there. The Arab Legion is a long-service volunteer army; there are no conscripts, and the volunteers come to stay. 9 Regiment was always well over 800 strong, and sometimes passed the 900 mark. More than half the officers and men were not in fact Jordanians, but came from Iraq, Saudi Arabia or Syria. The fame of Glubb Pasha and the renown of the Legion had long since spread to the remotest tribes.

The average length of service of all ranks in 9 Regiment was calculated to be about four and a half years. A sergeant with less than ten years' service was extremely rare; indeed it was hard to reach the rank of lance-corporal with less than four years' service. Many of the soldiers joined as beardless boys, but it was not possible to calculate the average age of the men, because they were extremely vague as to their date of birth. Lieutenant Hammad Faleh, the oldest officer, was reckoned to be about forty-three, because his earliest memory was of a bitter cold winter, possibly that of 1917! A little vague. Over half the Regiment were married, for the bedu, and indeed the Arabs as a race, take unto themselves wives at an early age.

In 9 Regiment fully 90 per cent of the men were bedouin. Only the clerks, signallers, storemen, sweepers, builders, cooks, dhobis, medical orderlies and buglers were haderi. In general, any task which the bedu could not bring themselves to do fell to the lot of the townsmen or the fellah. The bedu do not object to driving — indeed those who fail to become N.C.O.s try hard to get into the M.T. They would not mind being signallers, but those with sufficient education for the job become N.C.O.s.

There was no attempt to put men from the same tribe into the same platoon or company. Quite the contrary, in fact, for that might well encourage nepotism, which is regarded as a virtue by the Arabs. Some knowledge of the various tribes was invaluable to a commanding officer. If a company commander recommended the promotion of a sergeant, it was as well to know whether they were both from, let us say, the Beni Sakhr or not.

Two people are certainly important to a commanding officer: his adjutant and his driver. In these offices I was well served. Saoud Rashdan joined the Arab Legion from the French army after being captured in 1941. In 1948 he served as a sergeant in Glubb Pasha's bodyguard, and by 1951 had risen to the rank of lieutenant. He commanded No. 3 Company at first, but as he did well on his courses, was a cheerful, good-tempered person, who knew his drill and was well turned out, it was clear that he ought to become my Adjutant. It was objected that he was not very highly educated, which was really a great advantage, for he was not tempted to sit in his office. The Chief Clerk, Fuad Shahin, was perfectly capable of handling the paper work. Saoud proved a splendid Adjutant. For one thing, being a bachelor, he was always present with the Regiment; for another he had a wonderful "old boy net", not only in the Regiment but in Brigade, Division and Qiada.[3] He knew how to make the bedouin work, and like working; when to give them sweets, and when to wield the big stick. Their characters were well known to him; he knew the faint-hearted and the idle; the brave and the diligent. If I happened to be in a bad temper, he knew that too.

---

[3] Headquarters: i.e. H.Q. Arab Legion.

When I first joined the Arab Legion it took me some time to find a Land-Rover driver who had my confidence. James Watson's driver was a polite and pleasant person, but too pious for my taste. On one occasion when I wanted to move off he was engaged in his somewhat lengthy orisons. Salim Matar suited me well enough. Doughty would have called him an elfish and perfidious bedouin: unfortunately he fell foul of the Adjutant and the R.S.M., and had to go. Several others came and went. Eventually I told my staff that I wanted the best driver they had, and was tired of saying so.

"What think you of Juma'a," I heard Salameh say. Issa and the rest looked very dubious, but in due course there appeared a bedouin of more than normal height, erect, arrogant, with a rather Central Asian look. His turnout was pretty good, quite unlike a driver, and that was a pleasant change in itself. I thought he would suit me well enough, and he drove me from then on — until I reached Amman airport on 13th March this year, 1956.

He was from the Beni Atieh. In his youth he had shot his brother-in-law who had killed his wife, and come up to Palestine, where he engaged in smuggling. This had not been a great success, so he joined the Jeish and served with 1 Regiment in 1948. At first he was a bren-gunner, but later had been sent to Jerusalem as a sniper, and had spent some time shooting from the Old City walls into the Jewish Quarter. Afterwards when that had been cleared he was sent to the Palestine Police Depot and from the tower of a building which is now the U.N.R.W.A. Headquarters, he used to snipe at the Israelis in the Sanhedriya. He told me he had hit eighteen. Be that as it may, I can only say that he had eyes like field-glasses, and was a first-class shot.

He was one of the cadre of 9 Regiment and rose to be a section commander. However, being unlettered, he had no chance of promotion so he went to the transport, and on his return from a course at the driving school he took over my Land-Rover.

Juma'a did not think much of reading and writing. Various scholars, including Ahmed Qasim, offered to teach him, but he avoided lessons; I suppose he thought that reading would only spoil his eyesight. Nevertheless he managed to pass his promotion exam to corporal. I could not understand this, for three of the subjects were written, indeed when he asked to be entered I said to him "But you can't read".

"Never mind — at least I shall pass the drill, the tactics and the weapon training."

"As you wish."

He attended the exam, and passed in all subjects — education, administration and military law included!

Light dawned when the results appeared. There was in the Regiment a clerk called Ali Abbas Ireqat; he was a very fine Arabic typist, although otherwise an unsoldierly person. Fuad, the Chief Clerk, once caught me in an unguarded moment and persuaded me to make him a lance-corporal, and in due course Ali had the effrontery to present himself at a promotion exam. To everyone's surprise and astonishment he failed in ALL subjects. Had he failed in drill, tactics and weapon training one could have understood it … it seems he was afraid of Juma'a.

Saoud Rashdan was not the only one in 9 Regiment who had served in the French army. There were at least two others, Corporal Saoud Eid, the best shot in the Regiment, and Ameer Thiab, Juma'as aged father-in-law, whose name means "Prince of Wolves". Ameer still had two medals which he had won there, but the ribbons had long since vanished. Messrs.

Baldwins of Robert Street, Adelphi, were able to identify these gongs for him, and sent him a piece of the ribbon!

James Watson was a keen rifle shot and in 1952, thanks to his efforts, the Regiment won the Lash Cup, an enormous silver trophy for the best team at the Arab Legion Rifle Meeting. There were a number of good shots in the Regiment, but it was evident from his letter-book that James had had little support from the officers, except Salameh who was in the team. It seemed to me that the Arab officers ought to organize the shooting for themselves, and I asked Salameh to take this on. He explained that he was due to go on an English language course at midsummer, and suggested that Saleem Qurani should be responsible, to which I agreed. In 1953 the Hashemite Regiment contrived to win the cup, but it returned to the Regiment in the following year.

The swimming team also was run by the Arab officers, first by Shaman Etayek and later by Muhamad Awwad el Harbi. The Regiment always managed to get into the Jeish finals, a rare feat for a bedouin unit, although it must be admitted that there was a sprinkling of haderi clerks and signallers in the team.

The bedouin soldiers are devout and pious people. They are not pompous about their religion, wearing it lightly, nor are they great theologians, but they cling to the chief tenets of the Moslem faith. The Prophet has made clear the five duties incumbent on the true Moslem: he must bear witness that God is Greatest and that Muhamad is his Prophet. He must pray five times a day. He must give alms to the poor, fast during Ramadan, and make the pilgrimage to Mecca if he has the means.

In our camp at Khaw stands a simple stone-build mosque, paid for partly by the soldiers, and partly by a grant from the

Pasha. Salameh Etayek organized this in Watson's day, and the mosque was built while I was commanding. Often at midday I have seen half the Regiment praying there. Sometimes when the Regiment was on guard duties at the Palace, I have been woken in the cool of the morning by the shrill cry of some jundi doing duty as Muezzin, for Sheikh Ahmed Konaish, our Imam, used to train some of them in these duties.

The great fast of Ramadan, which lasts for thirty days, plays havoc with the military life of Arabia. It is forbidden to drink water or take food from two hours before sunrise until sunset, and this rule is strictly observed even when the fast falls in the summer season. Sexual intercourse, smoking, the use of medicines, all are forbidden by day. Even nursing mothers must fast. A bona fide traveller, marching from dawn to dusk, is exempt, but gains virtue if he fasts during his journey. Soldiers in the front line, toiling at the defences or constantly patrolling, are usually granted a dispensation, which has little effect for they are too pious to risk taking it. My first year in Jordan we were at Khaw; I was new to the Legion, and I let things take their course. In my second year we were at Jerusalem with much work on our hands, the men had dispensation, and they earned their pay, but many still kept the fast.

Sheikh Abdul Rezegh occupied a unique position in the Legion; he was a Holy Man who had attached himself to 9 Regiment. In its camp at Khaw, just behind the Officers' Mess stood his small two-roomed house, erected it is said thanks to the piety of Major Hassan ed Din, O.C. Records. In it he kept a platoon of cats which he loved dearly. Money, females, photography, all were abhorrent to him. He fed with the officers, and every now and then was re-clothed by them. He never spoke — or hardly ever — for he was vowed to silence.

It was said that he had once made a prophecy for King Abdulla and that when it came true, lesser persons pestered him to foretell the future for them. Disgusted — or perhaps just wise — he determined never to speak again. Once, when he fell ill, he was heard to call for food and water and, according to Glubb Pasha, he uttered remarkable comments when his finger was caught in the door of a motor car. But generally he conversed by signs, and some of the Regiment, especially Fuad, the Chief Clerk, were first-class interpreters in his strange language. For example, a benevolent smile towards a visiting General, accompanied by a slow motion of the right arm, as if administering a flogging, signified unqualified approval of the embarrassed victim. Another series of symbols meant "It is time you wrote to Qiada again, and told them to add a Minaret to the Regimental Mosque". When he leaned forward and touched Abdulla Dahil's epaulettes, this meant "What about making Abdulla a second lieutenant?"

Whenever some religious feast came round, not an infrequent occurrence in Jordan, he would appear at my office with a disarming smile and a series of field-signals, which, as I knew only too well, meant "Lend me a Land-Rover that I may go up to Jerusalem to pray." "*Wellahi*, it is not possible. Then will the Brigadier become mad." But such prevarication did not serve. The Brigadier's mental state was nothing to one who was himself not altogether as other men.

When I joined I was surprised to find that roughly 2 per cent of the Regiment were Greek Orthodox Christians. They were a mixed bag and included one colour-sergeant, the medical sergeant and one of his section, a storeman, a dhobi, one of the quartermaster's clerks, two drivers, four signallers, two masons, an ironer and a labourer. They were mostly East Bankers from Huson, near Irbid, Kerak and Amman. One of the signallers,

Issa Moussa, which being translated means Jesus Moses, was a good swimmer and a good soldier, who supported his widowed mother and his brothers and sisters, four in number if I remember rightly. But on the whole I was not impressed by my co-religionists.

There was little serious crime in a bedouin regiment, the chief offence being absence without leave, which as often as not was due to the soldier failing to calculate the amount of time needed for travelling to and from his home. An application for leave was seldom refused, and so this crime was really quite unnecessary. There were occasional cases of insolence, though I do not recall any instances of striking a superior, and there were occasional quarrels.

Very few of the bedouin drink alcohol, but in 9 Regiment we did have a second lieutenant and a colour-sergeant who were addicted to the bottle. Neither of them was any good, and I eventually succeeded in getting rid of both.

The usual minor offences common to military life were sometimes met in the Legion. The bedouin lost articles of kit, wandered around Zerqa with his collar undone, or drove his vehicle too fast just as other soldiers do, but rather less often.

All Military Police charges had to be tried by the Commanding Officer, and I also made it a rule that anyone who was absent without leave was to be brought up in front of me. When I took over I found that all other cases were disposed of by Salameh, for that had been the practice when he was Adjutant. I considered that the less important cases ought to be tried by the company commanders, and by checking the minor offence reports myself, a task which in the British army is usually delegated to the second-in-command, I tried to ensure that there were no gross miscarriages of justice.

A commanding officer in the Legion had rather greater powers of punishment than his counterpart in our service. He could send a man to prison for two months and at the same time recommend his discharge from the Jeish (Army). In the British army twenty-eight days detention is the maximum that a C.O. may give. The prisoner did not have the option of being tried by Court Martial, rather than accept his C.O.'s award. Confinement to Barracks was not much of a punishment to a bedouin soldier, who liked nothing better than sitting around in his hut talking to "the brethren". Minor offences were therefore punished by fines, which were deducted from the soldier's monthly pay, and went into a central fund. Company commanders were at first inclined to award fines of one or two days' pay, which, of course, caused the finance branch at Qiada more trouble than they were worth. The minimum fine was therefore set at three days' pay, more trivial offences being punished by fatigues or extra guards.

Trials could be puzzling to a British C.O. They were conducted outwardly on much the same lines as in the British army, but the culprit had no right of appeal. He was marched in by the R.S.M., without belt or head-dress, and escorted by another soldier of equal rank, with drawn bayonet in his right hand. Presumably the escort was supposed to stick this into the prisoner should he attack me, but after a time we got the Mark IV rifles with their short bayonets, and the escorts looked so ridiculous with these skewers in their hands that I abolished that part of the ceremonial.

The Adjutant read out the charge, and the prisoner pleaded "Not Guilty", at least I cannot recall any instance of one pleading otherwise. There was a magnanimous rule, dating from Watson's day, by which anyone who was caught by the Military Police automatically got seven days' fine for blackening the face of the Regiment. That simplified matters. In calculating the punishment the man's personal file was a help; if he had a clean sheet I usually felt disposed to leave it so. If he had already been up in front of me for a similar offence he was due for a double dose. When I was in doubt Salameh, Saoud, Issa or Khdayer would sometimes, whether invited or not, contribute illuminating sidelights on a case. But sometimes the Arab officers were dumb, knowing the man to be guilty, yet for some obscure motive of their own trying to shield him from the consequences of his actions. After a time one sensed this. The solution was simple: thunder followed by a heavy sentence. The wretched man would be taken off to prison and for ten minutes or so peace would prevail in the office, but soon there would be mutterings in the veranda, and after a time some officer, who felt himself to be privileged — Hammad perhaps — came in to speak for half a dozen others, all urging me to reverse my doom. I would pretend to put them off saying:

"*Wellahi*. You must think me mad. He is no soldier. Two months prison is not enough."

In the process of changing my mind the prisoner's friends could be trusted to reveal the true facts and a somewhat more lenient sentence might be arrived at. The officers would leave contented, and Ahmed Qasim, who enjoyed these little dramas, would say to me "Allah! Khurb Shaitanak!" "God overthrow the devil that is within you!"

I have mentioned that in the Legion a commanding officer when condemning a man to imprisonment, could at the same time recommend his discharge. If a C.O. wrote to Qiada and said that in his opinion So-and-So was useless and should leave the army, there was every probability that his opinion would be accepted, whether the soldier was in prison or not. Of course, if the C.O. had signed a report a few months previously saying that the man was "above average", and "suitable for accelerated promotion", his recommendation might not be followed. It would be suspected that the man's platoon or company commander had "fixed" him as the result of some private feud.

When a soldier's contract expired the C.O. could refuse to renew it, or if he felt doubtful, he could renew it for one year only. I used to interview all time-expired men, and look through their personal files, before signing them on again, for it was the exception for a soldier to wish to leave the Jeish.

At one time a certain number of men used to be sent each month to the reserve, though only men from the Jordanian tribes were effected, as it would have been impossible to call up reservists from Iraq or Saudi Arabia. The men selected for the reserve were not usually outstandingly smart or bright, and some of them were illiterate; the Regiment suffered little from their departure. There was another class of reservists, consisting of older men, and those with minor disabilities, who were destined to work on the Lines of Communication in time of war.

It will be seen that the commanding officer had every opportunity to improve the personnel of his regiment, and that there was really no need to carry passengers. 9 Regiment, like any other, was none the worse for a little pruning.

It was customary for a bedouin soldier, who felt "wronged" or otherwise "obliged", to seek an interview with his commanding officer, or even with "Abuna el Kebir".[4] Then he would hang about outside the office, or if repelled by Salim Hussein or another, would visit my house under cover of darkness, "ed dinya leil" as they say, "the world night", a

---

[4] Glubb Pasha.

delightful phrase. Omer, my batman, would appear and say that So-and-So was in the tent, where Juma'a and he slept, and after a time some bedouin would be ushered into the dining-room.

"Good evening."

"Good evening."

"How are you?"

"How is your colour?"

"How is your health?"

During this fusillade of questions as often as not the bedu would peer at you, to see if you had deteriorated since the last meeting!

"Badein? And then?"

"*Wellahi!* You are our father. Your presence is enough, but *Wellahi*, I am obliged/wronged ...." and after these formalities out would come a long tale, told with such fervour that I was lucky if I got one word in four. No matter. The facts of the case could be established by supplementary questions. As often as not it was a simple problem which merely involved granting the man a normal interview in office hours. Sometimes it was more complicated, as when some hapless jundi's house was used by an officer for clandestine interviews with the wife of another, the officer alternately threatening the soldier with discharge, and cajoling him with promises of an education course and subsequent promotion. To send for a bedouin to the office, and question him through an interpreter, is a very good way of getting no information. Needless to say the men were forbidden to seek one out in this way, but perhaps fortunately, this was not one of the rules they obeyed.

A typical case of a bedu who thought himself wronged, although not one of 9 Regiment, was that of Naif Mireid, a Harb and a relation of Naqib Hleyil Mfadhi, who was acting as

R.S.M. at the time. In 1954 this man was posted as a driver to the 1st Field Regiment, where there had always been a few bedouin, but he did not settle down well and he told Hleyil that he was the only bedu in the battery and was oppressed — there were in fact half a dozen others, who bombarded the C.O. with applications to be transferred, which were duly forwarded to Qiada. Naif was assured that his application was among them, but he had his doubts on the subject, and although he was under arrest at the time for some other offence, he left his vehicle outside the battery, and departed to Amman taking his sten and ammunition with him. He sought sanctuary in the Pasha's garden, but the Military Police managed to extricate him and take him back to Palestine. A few days later he informed his C.O. that he had no right to prevent his seeing the Pasha, saying that there was no justice for a bedu in that regiment. To which the C.O. replied that if that was so someone outside the regiment had better try the case, and remanded him for Court Martial.

I relate this incident merely to show some of the odd notions that the bedouin sometimes get into their heads, their impulsiveness, and the way they can sometimes brood over and dramatize "wrongs", at least in part imaginary. This man had been posted from a unit where he had friends, to a regiment which was almost 100 per cent haderi and went sour. In that frame of mind a bedu reckons that King's Regulations apply to all the others but not to him.

As another example of the occasional cussedness of the bedu I would mention that while the Regiment was on guard duties in 1953, Eid Hweimil, who was really a very passable N.C.O., got it into his head that the ration meat was not properly killed as an orthodox Moslem was entitled to expect. He therefore refused to eat his rations, and lived on his pay — that is to say on what remained after his relations had visited him. This I only discovered because I noticed that his face had become covered in blemishes. He steadfastly refused to eat the rations and, as I was equally determined not to support him from the canteen fund, we reached an impasse. Fortunately he was despatched to the Cadet School and his apparently insoluble problem went with him.

Towards the end of 1953 we lost quite a good, battle-tried N.C.O., for very similar reasons. He was Abdul Aziz Irshaid, who was one of the senior corporals and had passed his promotion exam. He went on a Junior Drill Course and failed to get a grading because he disliked being corrected. Things came to a head during the final drill examination when he was being tested by the Senior Arab Instructor, assisted by R.S.M. Jones of the Welsh Guards. He was checked several times because he was teaching the lesson wrongly, and in the end he lost his temper, and told the Senior Instructor that he had not wanted to attend the course in the first place! He was told to rejoin his squad.

It was comparatively rare for a N.C.O. to fail a course altogether, for the students were carefully selected from among those who had a good chance of getting an average grading. I therefore decided not to promote Abdul Aziz, and he decided to go home to the Nejd, and thus the Legion lost an N.C.O. who, though a stupid old man, was, by repute, very brave. I do not really like temperamental N.C.O.s so I was not unduly depressed.

The "old boy net" is pretty highly developed among the Arabs. I have mentioned the case of Naif Mireid, which I would never have known about had Hleyil Mfadhi not been his relation. Another instance was an attempt made in April 1954, to transfer, without replacement be it said, Jundi Signaller

Khalid Eid to the Royal Signals for training as a radio-mechanic. The Chief Signal Officer told me that he only knew of his existence because he was a friend of his corporal driver! As the Signal Platoon was then six short of establishment, and four of the signallers had managed to fail their proficiency tests, my answer was not particularly helpful.

Another classic example of the use of the "old boy net", dates from about the same period. Every year several names were put forward for awards in the 4th and 5th classes of the Istiqlal. Usually one other rank only received the 5th Class, and I was surprised when I found that it was allotted to a corporal who, though a very good chap, was not the first choice. It was some time before this mystery was cleared up, but after a time it came to light — through my own "old boy net" — that one of my officers had visited Lt.-Col. Khaled es Sahen, the president of the appropriate board, and had urged that this N.C.O., a friend of his, should be the person honoured.

The bedouin has his own ways of being rude to people. "Your Father! And the Father of he that brought you!" he cries, a phrase of shameful significance. If he is angry he wraps his shemagh over his face so that only his smouldering eyes are visible. Shouting, swearing and roaring, particularly if directed at an individual, though it may serve to wake him up, he finds distressing. It was said of Glubb Pasha that if someone had incurred his displeasure, he would merely ignore him, answering none of the customary greetings. This blackened the offender's face very effectively. The Arabic code of politeness, part of their Byzantine heritage, seems somewhat formal and even hollow to the Westerner: to the Arab the manners of Englishmen and Americans too often seem uncouth. But the bedouin, while preserving the forms of courtesy, cannot conceal the warmth and sympathy that usually lurk beneath their quaint phrases. The tradition of hospitality is with them a living thing, and it is a blessed hour that brings the guest, whether known or unknown, whether he is merely the C.O. who must be lured from his inspections to drink tea with "the brethren" in their barrack-room, or the G.O.C. visiting the Regiment, who must be the guest of honour at a mensif. The attached officer from the Canal Zone, the second-in-command returning from a course in England, the visitor staying with the colonel, all will be feasted, not once but many times. If you do not like eating sheep, steer clear of the bedouin.

Many of the phrases used among the bedouin are little used among the haderis. Once on a bitter night during manoeuvres, the blankets and greatcoats arrived late from B echelon. Fuad, a Moslem from Bethlehem, was one of those who went round giving them out. When he had done he came and reported to me, full of merriment. He told me: "They were saying to me 'God lengthen your days'. 'God recommend you' and 'God whiten your face'."

The bedouin are the most delightful people to serve with and to meet in the ordinary way. They are not unlike the Highlanders in the days of the '15 and '45; with their tails up and with leaders they trust they will fight admirably for short periods. They have not yet had to put up with bombing or shelling such as commonly fell to the lot of the British soldier in the last war, and I personally would do anything I could to avoid committing them to a slogging match. That is not to say that I think they would fail under those conditions, but their temperament, tradition and previous experience does not fit them for that style of warfare.

At the worst the bedouin can be stupid, sullen and fit for nothing, but there are few of this type. At the best they are cheerful, willing and hardy soldiers, ready to go anywhere and try anything.

CHAPTER III: TAKING OVER

I took over command of 9 Regiment on 10th April, 1953, with the good intention of taking things quietly for the first few months, until I knew a little about the people, and until they had had time to get used to me. Looking through the letters with which I bombarded the second-in-command, and the company commanders during the period before I knew enough Arabic to give them my orders verbally, I see how little I succeeded in living up to this resolve. The personnel and training of the 3-inch mortar platoon; education; idle sentries; internal security; sizing of a dismounted unit; weapon training; turnout; the fitting of greatcoats; and the distribution of the petrol available were only a few of the subjects which evidently claimed attention in those first few weeks.

Early in April the Regiment departed to Merka for a month to practise for the Arab Legion Day Parade. Salameh Etayek and three hundred men, including the whole of the rifle companies and nearly all the officers, were to take part in this spectacle. H.Q. and support companies stayed at Khaw. It seemed that British officers were not required on these occasions, and so I was able to spend most of my time learning Arabic and planning training against the day when the Regiment should return.

Muhamad Mohsin, a dear old gentleman who commanded Support Company, was left in charge of the rear party. In 1948 he had been hit in the jaw by a 3-inch mortar, but otherwise he knew very little about heavy weapons. This senior bedouin captain, Muhamad, a Harb from the Nejd, was really about thirty-seven; he had joined the camelry in 1939 but transferred to 1 Regiment in 1941. Twice wounded, in Iraq (1941) and in Palestine (1948), when as he himself told me — and presumably he should know — he had been recommended for a Gallantry Medal, which had been given to someone else of the same name. He had also fought in Syria. His wife, surprisingly enough, was a non-bedouin lady. Muhamad Bey was really senior to Salameh Etayek, the second-in-command, but he accepted this position loyally, for, to do him justice, he never claimed to be a leader of military thought. From 1940 to 1944 I had served in No. 3 Commando, which I had commanded for rather more than a year. It was inevitable that to a certain extent my ideas and my standards were still those of my Commando days. The bedouin were volunteers, and a certain amount of selection was possible in the Legion. Although I had become perhaps a little more tolerant than I had been ten years earlier, when after all there was a war on, I doubted whether friendliness was quite enough, at least as far as the officers were concerned. I wondered whether Muhamad Mohsin would stay the course.

The best of the bedouin would make very good Commandos for they are individualists, but at the same time smart and well behaved. They are active, hardy and quick in the uptake. In fact their chief handicap is lack of education, but although we worked long and hard to teach the men to read and write I am far from believing that an illiterate is necessarily a bad private soldier. It seemed to me as I began to get to know 9 Regiment that in many ways its men were not unlike those I had served with in the old Commando days. They were cheerful, and independent; they did not get lost on training — in finding his way about the Arab is more than a match for the British soldier — they did not get bored or demand a lot of looking after. If there was a bed they slept on it: if there was no bed they slept on the floor. Soldiers who want a lot of welfare are not very useful. These men were quite happy so long as someone in the section had a Primus stove. When the day's work was done they would sit round and gossip, while one of the brethren brewed tea and passed it round in little glasses. If a guest came so much the better, it was a blessed hour. It might be a friend on leave from another regiment, or particularly around pay-day, which with them is only once each month, it might be a relation come to collect a few dinars to take back to the family. As they talked they cleaned their equipment, or toiled at their copybooks.

When I commanded 3 Commando I used to keep on my desk a book with the names of all the officers and N.C.O.s in it, and their particulars. Hardly a day went by that I did not read this great work, and ponder how to be rid of the passengers, and advance those who were brave and diligent. When he left Watson had handed over a similar volume, which I studied daily for many months. It was gradually borne in on me that, due to its rapid expansion, the Arab Legion had a number of pretty inadequate officers and N.C.O.s, though the soldiers were splendid. Clearly the Regiment would never be really first class while people of this sort remained. Bedouins are a kindly and tolerant race and it was abundantly clear that if anyone was going to do the weeding it would have to be me. I set myself to get to know all the officers and N.C.O.s and as many of the soldiers as possible, not only with the object of getting rid of the duds, but so as to bring on those who had the light of battle in their eyes.

Since the Regiment was away at Merka I had time to get down to learning the language. I do not claim to have a very great knowledge of Arabic, nevertheless I was able to make myself reasonably well understood, and indeed it was essential for the C.O. of a bedouin regiment to know some Arabic because very few of the officers knew any English. I had a very good interpreter, Ahmed Qasim, a Palestinian sergeant from Acre district, and my Chief Clerk, Fuad Shahin, might pass as a second-class interpreter. Some of the signallers and clerks spoke a little English, but practically none of the bedouin other ranks knew any.

Ahmed Qasim was my teacher. In Watson's day he had always had his desk in the C.O.'s office, and this arrangement we continued. Anything I wanted to know he wrote down for me in English script, and I gradually built up a vocabulary. He taught me the words of command in Arabic as we watched Izzat Hassan, the newly promoted Qaid of 6 Regiment, drilling the contingent for the Arab Legion Day Parade at Merka. Morris Brightman, in an unguarded moment, lent me a most valuable book from which the Palestine Police used to teach Arabic to their British constables.

One morning in the office Ahmed said: "There is an examination in colloquial Arabic on 28th May. Of course, you will not want to try this time …"

"Put my name down."

"But, Sir, you will fail, and then your face will be blackened, and mine also."

I wanted my two shillings a day, and in due course I presented myself. I knew full well that the board, which consisted of the Chief Education Officer, Major Saleem Karachi, alias Abu William, and Captains Abdulla Bitar and Nicodeme, would wonder why I was appearing only two months after arrival, and being only human were practically bound to ask me how it was. I therefore prepared a long speech explaining this interesting point, and when the time came it was merely a matter of turning on the gramophone.

Ahmed and I were both pleased. I got my language pay, and he was able to go around saying what a clever teacher he was. I am compelled to admit that the Board on that occasion were not sufficiently hard hearted to fail anybody.

His Majesty King Hussein, who as yet had not been crowned, arrived from the United Kingdom on 6th April. A Guard of Honour from the Regiment was to meet him at the airport and so I drove to Merka in the morning, only to find that the King's arrival had been postponed until the afternoon. The Regiment was in a tented camp, and after having a look round I stayed to lunch with the officers. The King arrived late in the afternoon, inspected the Guard of Honour, which was quite good, and then held a brief reception in one of the hangars. Ministers, Sheikhs and officers filed past and were introduced. Glubb Pasha asked me whether I had been in, and himself presented me to the King.

While the main body of the Regiment was away, the running team remained at Khaw training for the final of the Arab Legion Cross Country Competition which was held there on the afternoon of 16th April. Six units took part, including such formidable opponents as the Arab Legion Training Centre, the Cadet School, and the Engineers. Two other infantry regiments had reached the final, 6 and 7, the latter also being bedouin.

James Watson, who had long held the British Army record for putting the weight, was very keen on all kinds of athletics, and had built up a strong regimental team. The star turn was Hassan Atallah, known as "Abu Sibil", "Father of the Pipe". Unfortunately his fame had spread to 7 Regiment's team, and when they saw a lean and bearded bedouin loping along with a pipe in his mouth they ran up to him and cried, "Are you Abu Sibil?" He replied that he was, whereupon they threw him to the ground and ran on over his prostrate body! This horrible story was related to me afterwards by the outraged members of our team, anxious to explain why they only got second place. 7 Regiment were first.

In the absence of the main body the rear party made a start with building married quarters, which were made of mud brick. A grant was given by Qiada for the purchase of materials and the units did the rest. There were three or four builders and a carpenter on the strength of each regiment, but most of the work was done by the soldiers. It was soon found that it was extremely inconvenient to change labourers each day and so about thirty men were selected from among the older soldiers, who were nearing the time for their discharge, and these worked away at the quarters. Curiously enough these men, who would have refused to try and learn the bagpipes and would have mutinied rather than be laundrymen, made no objection to becoming builders, for though most bedouin live in tents they appreciate houses. After a time they became adept at treading the mud and straw together, and pouring the mixture into the wooden moulds. The bricks were baked in the sun just as in Biblical times.

The quarters were built in blocks of four. Each had two living rooms, besides a kitchen and the usual offices, the whole being surrounded by a yard. The carpenter was an idle rogue, and the doors and windows took a long time making. The rest of the work progressed according to the strictness or otherwise of the N.C.O. in charge. When Naqib Salim Hussein was present there was progress; if Naib Muhamad Imfeileh was there the men usually rested.

These houses were much sought after and great care had to be exercised to see that they were fairly allotted. Abdulla Dahil, the senior resident, was made mukhtar of the village, and held responsible for its cleanliness and good order. A sentry had to be placed at the water point which supplied the families, as all sorts of refugees and people in no way connected with the army would drive down their donkeys, laden with jerricans, to fill up. The bedouin being hospitable people hardly knew how to resist these, or any other beggars that came to the camp. Feisal Mite'b, our provost corporal, made constant war on these unwanted neighbours, sallying forth unexpectedly on his motorcycle and driving them away with threats and curses.

Two officers' quarters had been built earlier and were occupied by Salameh and Muhamad Mohsin. Abu Ghazi's family lived in Amman, Salim Bakhet had a quarter in Zerqa Camp, while Abu Mudhish and a number of other officers rented houses in Zerqa town. Said Saleh, of fellah origin, had a small house and some well-watered land near the bridge, which he spent his spare time cultivating. Khalaf Ghassib's family lived at Mafraq, and he like many of the officers, married and single, lived in the Mess.

Many of the soldiers' families accompanied the Regiment wherever it went. Some would rent houses in Zerqa, or Et Tur, or wherever we might be, while the others lived in their black tents. At Khaw there were always upwards of seventy tents pitched in a wadi within about half a mile of the camp.

On 1st May, the eve of King Hussein's accession, a Service of Intercession was held in the Church of the Redeemer, Amman, which was attended by a great number of the British officers. Next day the King came to the throne, and the Arab Legion Day Parade was held at Merka Airfield on 3rd May in honour of his accession.

His Majesty was then about eighteen years of age, and attracted all the sympathy and affection that a young and handsome King can command. His extreme shyness, which might have seemed a disadvantage in a monarch of maturer years, almost made him more attractive. Educated in Alexandria and later at Harrow and Sandhurst, he spoke perfect English. He had acquired a taste not unnatural in one of his age for piloting his own aircraft, and driving at considerable speeds in high-powered motor cars — a trait which may have distressed his ministers, but seemed refreshingly natural to more ordinary mortals. A slim and handsome figure in his field-marshal's uniform, he was hailed with enthusiasm as he drove on to the parade ground escorted by red-coated lancers. To the accompaniment of twenty-one guns and the massed bugles of the division the parade gave a royal salute.

Glubb Pasha handed over the parade and after His Majesty's inspection the units marched past the royal dais, cavalry, camelry, national guards, colour parties from every arm of the service, 6 Regiment and then at last my own new command, with Salameh Etayek marching at their head. At the rear, after more colour parties, came armoured cars and artillery.

Almost the most impressive moment was the trot past of the two troops of the Desert Patrol, the bedouin with their red sashes and their flowing white sleeves adding a touch of barbaric splendour. No words of mine can describe the disdainful expression on the senior camel's face!

Twenty officers, twenty-four senior N.C.O.s and 300 men formed the 9 Regiment contingent, marching past in six companies. Among those who received medals were Rais Abdul Rahman Mustafa, the Quartermaster, and Naqib Abdulla Modhi, an outstanding N.C.O. These, of course, had been selected by my predecessor.

After the Parade the soldiers returned to Khaw, and their hard work was rewarded with two days' leave.

Her Majesty Queen Elizabeth had been represented at King Hussein's Coronation by H.R.H. The Duke of Gloucester, who visited units in the Zerqa area on 6th May. In the evening, after a horrible afternoon of wind and dust, the Massed Bands beat retreat in his honour on the parade ground in Zerqa Camp and gave us a fine selection of "British" martial music, including "Les Huguenots" and the slow march from "Scipio".

Towards the middle of May the fast of Ramadan began, an exhausting period for the ninety-eight per cent of the Regiment who were Moslems. Working hours were officially cut down, but still we managed to get most of the men through their annual musketry course. During the earlier part of the month we were continually being called upon to provide Guards of Honour for V.I.P.s who had come to the Coronation, and large detachments to cordon the aerodrome. No. 1 Company was detached to H.5 to combat the locusts, and one way and another we had little opportunity for any tactical training. Moreover the annual administrative inspection was in the offing. It was carried out by Brigadier McCully, on 7th and 8th June, and blew over satisfactorily.

Ramadan ended on 13th June, and was followed by the usual holiday, Eid el Fitr. By this time my car was due to arrive at Aqaba and taking Juma'a and Awwad I drove down in a Land-Rover to fetch it. I left Zerqa at 4 p.m. on 14th June and arrived at Aqaba at 3.30 a.m. the next morning. The *Empire Chubb* was not yet in sight and so next day, accompanied by Kenneth Beauchamp, a lieutenant-colonel from G.H.Q., I set off for Petra, the ancient capital of the Nabataean Kings.

We rode on horseback from the little village of Wadi Moussa, down through the wilderness towards the sheer cliffs which wall this city of tombs. Nothing in Petra is as impressive as its entrance through a gorge, at no point wider than six yards. We rode through the shadowy ravine, a high cleft where a score of resolute men could hold an army at bay, until suddenly the most perfect of all the tombs, the Khazneh, stood before us, rose-coloured in the morning sunshine. Khazneh means Treasury, but there is little doubt that this is really the rock-hewn burial place of some Nabataean King.

All day we wandered through the place, exploring the tombs, and climbing eventually to the Deir or Convent, from which we could see Wadi Arabah lying four thousand feet below us, the tomb of Aaron to the South, and away to the West the hills of Palestine.

Ramadan being over, at last we were able to get down to some serious training. It would be tedious indeed to describe the numerous exercises and demonstrations which we carried out in the summer of 1953. Platoon attacks, company attacks, night firing, digging exercises; manoeuvres when we acted as enemy to 10 Regiment, the usual round of battalion training. Still, I may be forgiven if I recall a few incidents, and it is particularly the night operations that I remember, for the Regiment was well-versed in the normal tactics of fighting in daylight and for that reason nothing of note has stayed in my mind.

There may well have been night attacks before Gideon's time but his is the first which is recorded in any detail. The story is well-known. How he selected three companies from his best-disciplined volunteers, and gave them special equipment: trumpets and lamps in pitchers. How in the middle watch the morale of the Midianites broke so that "the host ran, and cried and fled …" and "the Lord set every man's sword against his fellow." Who were these Midianites who "came up with their cattle and their tents … as grasshoppers for multitude; for both they and their camels were without number...''? They were the bedouin, who like locusts from the desert came in with their black tents, passed the fords of Jordan, somewhere near Beisan, and reached the plain of Esdraelon. This is not only the first detailed account of a night attack, it is also the first recorded instance of a long-range raid by camelry. These Midianites were mobile and therefore formidable, and they were sufficiently military to set a watch. Still their morale was not proof against a surprise night attack and broke when they heard the battle-cry: "The sword of the Lord and of Gideon." This battle fought between Mount Gilboa and the Hill of Moreh deserves attention. The Midianites, like any other soldiers, were worse than useless at night without discipline and training, and I now found myself in command of a Midianite regiment!

The country to the East of Jordan with the exception of Ajlun district is generally very open, low stony hills bounded to the East by desert and lava. If we were to move about in such country in war we would have to do most of our movement by night. The bedouin as individuals are extremely skilful at finding their way about. Without map or compass they will go great distances where Europeans would be lost in a few miles. With their excellent eyesight these people ought to be able to use the night as a weapon. Indeed in their raiding days they often used to advance on their enemy under cover of darkness, and rush his camp at dawn. Moving individuals, and moving a battalion with its support weapons are two different things. It was clear that we would have to do some night training.

We started with a simple exercise on the night of 22nd/23rd June. A platoon under Abdulla Modhi took up a defensive position around the six-arched bridge on the Hejaz railway, which lies between Zerqa, Khaw and Sukhne, a bridge, incidentally, which had been attacked by Lawrence in 1918.

Salameh Etayek with 1, 4 and Support Companies, less the anti-tank platoon, was to capture this objective, and hold it for half an hour while an imaginary demolition party destroyed the bridge. It was only a march of a few miles, and the aim was to practise the soldiers in moving quickly and quietly by night, taking up positions rapidly and brushing away light opposition.

Led by a fighting patrol under Muhamad Moazi, they advanced at a good speed, and without noise. They had no difficulty in finding their way. The enemy, bored by their long wait, passed the time in talking and coughing and were driven out after a short resistance. The mortars and Vickers kept up with the rest of the force; Salameh wasted no time in deploying the companies, and after half an hour the bridge was considered blown. So far so good, but all ranks now considered that they had done enough for one night, and withdrew towards camp highly delighted with themselves, discussing their adventures, and laughing at each other. A cigarette glowed in the ranks. At least they were enjoying themselves. I regretted my lack of Arabic, but cursed them in good English, and hoped that Ahmed Qasim was not translating my comments too literally.

Meanwhile, Abdulla Modhi, who was an active and enterprising person, passed the column and opened fire on No. 1 Company from a flank. Bedr Mansour with 2 Platoon returned the fire, and while he was doing so 1 Platoon, on its way home, marched across his front, between two fires! A very curious manoeuvre. As I drove home it seemed to me that the Regiment might profit from some more night training, but the bedouin soldier is quick to learn from his mistakes; and is moreover genuinely eager to please his commanders and to earn their praise. It was not long before night operations became their strong point.

On 27th June we had a brief visit from General Sir Cameron Nicholson, the Commander-in-Chief, Middle East Land Forces. A few days beforehand Brigade demanded a programme from us, and it was agreed that the General should be invited to inspect a Guard of Honour; look round one of the barrack rooms; watch the 3-inch mortar and Vickers platoons training; and then adjourn to see some of the soldiers firing their annual classification course on the range.

The R.S.M. toiled to produce a glistening guard; the Signals Platoon sweated blood beautifying their barracks; the platoons of Support Company drilled till they were ready to drop; and Salameh busied himself with the details of the range work.

At ten o'clock the General arrived at the gate of the camp. The Guard was really very good. Corporal Eid Hweimil, a lean wooden-faced Howeiti, produced "Salaam al Generral" from the pit of his stomach, and one of 10 Regiment's buglers, suitably disguised, blew the General Salute. All went well until we reached the range where it really went rather too well. A detail was firing when we arrived. Some of the forms lying on the firing point looked familiar: Tobash Nahar, Abbas Sari and Ingheimish Hamdan … It was a fine bright morning with no wind. From the butts they signalled bull after bull in rapid succession. The General turned to me, "Now tell me, is this one of your platoons, or have these men been picked?"

Our night training reached a climax in August when King Feisal of Iraq visited his cousin of Jordan. It was decided that they should see a demonstration of a battalion doing a night attack, and it fell to 9 Regiment to arrange this. A valley was chosen near Rukban, a little to the East of Zerqa. Needless to say this was lifted bodily from that excellent work "The Infantry Battalion in Battle"; according to John Harrison, late of the 16th Foot, "So long as you've got this little book, you can play the battalion like a piano." There was to be a commentary broadcast in Arabic by public address equipment, but unfortunately the draft was not quite long enough and eventually it was decided to fill it out by making the enemy commander put in some additional remarks.

The Regiment practised this demonstration several times by day, then by night, and lastly firing live ammunition. We had a Bofors firing tracer to show the centre line, and Vickers machine-guns firing tracer on the flanks. Countless made-up charges represented the barrage on the enemy position, and in their wire a knocked-out armoured car added a touch of realism.

The Kings arrived in the dusk walking up a specially prepared track to sit in a stand from which every rock and pebble had been removed. A panorama of the enemy position, a masterpiece by Donald Kennedy-Macgregor, lay on a table before them. Nearby Muhamad Mohsin sat in a slit trench pretending to be a battalion commander. Punctual to the second the commentator began to hold forth, the bogus guns boomed out, the enemy commander came on the air, at first confident, but later confused and despairing as the bedouin overran his mythical platoons.

Promotion examinations were a great feature of life in the Arab Legion and occupied quite a lot of one's time. In 1953 a C.O. could not even promote a private to lance-corporal although this was changed later. The promotion examinations for junior N.C.O.s were organized by brigade headquarters, and for senior N.C.O.s and officers by Division. Successful candidates were promoted if they were recommended by their commanding officers, and if their annual confidential reports, held at Qiada, were deemed satisfactory. This elaborate system was no doubt intended to check the nepotism, which is a feature of Arab life.

On 11th July, for the first time, I assembled a board to hold a promotion examination within the Regiment, in order to select lance-corporals. We added shooting to the compulsory subjects laid down by Qiada; for junior N.C.O.s who cannot shoot are a dead loss. As a result of this examination eleven soldiers were promoted at the beginning of August. Their names are before me as I write, and I knew them all well. The fourth now has "useless" written against his name, though he was a good shot and a passable private soldier. The rest have since become corporals and pretty good ones at that, so our system worked well enough.

Education necessarily took a prominent place in the training programme, for very few bedouin recruits could read and write when they joined the army. One period each day was normally set aside for education, and the companies had, if required, the assistance as teachers of signallers or clerks from H.Q. Company. Those of the soldiers who showed talent were then selected for education courses, which were run in the unit by N.C.O.s attached for the purpose. These men were enlisted as teachers and belonged to the Education Corps. Brigade Headquarters had an education officer who ran a school, not only for selected N.C.O.s and soldiers, but for their children. There were higher courses for officers, both in Arabic and in English, at the Arab Legion Training Centre. It will be seen that education was very highly organized in the Jeish, and very satisfactory results were achieved.

It was in August, as far as I remember, that Khalil Moussa, the Education Corporal, took it into his head to murder his sister. He stabbed her to death with a dagger in the streets of Amman, on the grounds that she had brought shame on the family by her immoral life. I was a little put out by this, for although we had several murderers in the Regiment none of them had committed their crimes whilst actually serving in the corps. The first result of this deed was that Fuad came to persuade me to lend twenty-five dinars for Khalil's defence. I naturally supposed he would swing for it, and was not disposed to raise a finger to save him. His father, an old lance-corporal in the Police Cavalry, put in an appearance. A good deal of weeping went on. He obviously had very little control over his offspring and, to console him, Ahmed Qasim and I paid a visit to the Mohatta prison in Amman, to see how Khalil was getting on.

Being in uniform we were admitted without difficulty, and ushered into an office just inside the iron barred gates. Coffee was brought. In the square yard numbers of convicts worked or sunned themselves. One wretched man had a heavy chain from his ankles to a belt at his waist: it was explained that he was violent. My hosts proudly showed me the gallows in a corner room, and we then returned to the office.

After an interval Khalil Moussa, smiling nervously but unrepentant, was brought in by a policeman. Clearly he thought that by taking the law into his own hands he had done a praiseworthy deed. When he was arrested his uniform and army kit had been handed in: we were able to arrange that his family should be allowed to bring him some clothing, for the Jordan nights are cold in October.

The Arabs do not look upon murders of this sort as a crime, and I dare say that Ahmed Qasim tactfully failed to tell Khalil that I expected him to be hanged. In fact he got off with two years in prison. He wrote to me in November thanking me for my visit and saying, "There will come a time when snow will melt and dust will clear, then I will rejoin the Arab Legion ..."

On 27th August we took over the guard duties from 3 Regiment. A strong detachment, 1 and 2 Companies, went to the Royal Palace, while 4 Company departed to Aqaba. 3 Company found numerous guards in Amman and Merka, at Qiada, the Mohatta, the Airport and the Main Hospital. Support Company was responsible for various guards in Zerqa, which included General Cooke's house, the main petrol store and both the civil and military prisons. Except for part of H.Q. very few men remained at Khaw, and most of my time was spent in travelling round to inspect the various detachments. On 15th September, the Regiment still being on guard duties, I went on leave to Cyprus, returning on 6th October.

One of the best sergeants was Ingheimish Hamdan of the Howeitat from Ma'an district, who had joined the Legion in 1941 and was probably in his late thirties; with his fine features and small well-trimmed beard he was one of the best-looking men in the Regiment. A dashing leader and a good shot he acted as C.S.M. of No. 4 Company; a charming man, though perhaps rather easy-going, he had a marked sense of humour. In December 1953 he decided to marry a second wife and came to me to borrow £25 from the Canteen Fund for the purpose. It was difficult to refuse, and indeed I did not succeed in doing so. Most Arabs have the sense to ask for twice as much as they really need, but Ingheimish stuck to his guns and insisted that £25, no more, no less, was the precise sum required to do things properly. In due course I was invited to the marriage feast. A few of the senior N.C.O.s and some of the men wore beards, which was permitted among the bedouin, although I do not recall any of the officers availing themselves of this privilege.

Nobody in 9 Regiment thought much of the efforts of higher authority to put an end to their practice of borrowing money from the Canteen Fund. The bedouin naturally supposes that a Qaid in his wisdom will treat each case on its merits. He believes that a General Order forbidding something that he wants to do merely applies to the rest of the regiment. The following masterpiece demanded my attention one morning soon after my return.

O.C. 9th Regt.

Sir,

Good morning,

My Coy. Clerk, Cpl. Hassan El Alami, is in need of 20 Dinars as his brother is sick in hospital.

I hope Sir to help him to can give him this money from Canteen Cash. And many thanks for you Sir for this fever to this person.

12.10.53
Yours,
Lt. Saoud Rashdan.

He got his loan — and in due course repaid it!

When I first met Saoud I noted in my diary that he was "a pleasant merry fellow" but by this time I had come to realize that he was far more than that. He administered his company well, he had shown that he could lay on a demonstration, and he and Salim Bakhet both had good results on the senior drill course which they attended during the summer.

By 17th October I had been six months in the Regiment, and felt I knew it well enough to reshuffle the pack. Saoud Rashdan became Adjutant, and Issa Abdulla replaced Musayeb Suleiman, who had followed Muhamad Mohsin but had not come up to expectations, in Support Company. Musayeb went to 1 Company and Abu Mudhish took over 3. These were not changes that I ever had reason to regret. Issa Abdulla had recently been promoted second-lieutenant when he was made

Adjutant. A quiet, calm, well-educated man, who had been selected for this appointment by Salameh Etayek partly because he was better educated than the other officers; he knew some English and improved his knowledge greatly as time went by, though I felt that he regarded himself as Salameh's adjutant rather than mine. I wanted someone who would help with the training but Issa preferred to spend his days in the office.

On the night of 14-15th October, 1953, a force of Israelis, perhaps a battalion strong, attacked the border village of Qibya. The garrison of six village guards was soon overcome, and in the massacre that followed fifty-two people were killed, men, women and children. Kamel Abdel Kader, commanding 10 Regiment did not appreciate what was happening, and the Israelis escaped without interference.

The people who survived began to remove their few belongings on donkeys or in any other way they could, and not until the village was practically empty did 10 Regiment appear and persuade them to return. A British officer, who was visiting the village on duty, found old Kamel standing by the roadside, completely shattered and saying: "Shu Korea? Shu Korea?" "What is Korea?"

In the five years of armistice there had been many border incidents, but never one on this scale. Several houses were actually blown up over the heads of their inhabitants, destroying whole families.

When the news of this incident came through I was with the H.Q … of 1 Brigade umpiring an exercise out in the desert North-East of Zerqa. The Regiment was still on guard duties.

Naturally this massacre caused a great outcry and the Government, not wishing to appear supine, ordered the Legion to Palestine. Divisional H.Q., two brigades, all the artillery and most of the armoured cars, moved off to the West Bank, leaving 9 Regiment in splendid isolation. My orders now came direct from Colonel Hutton, the Chief of Staff at Qiada.

No sooner had the Division disappeared than it became known that trouble was brewing in Amman, and I was ordered to report to Qiada at twelve o'clock on 20th October, for a conference. Colonel Walden, the commander of the Arab Legion Training Centre; Sir Patrick Coghill, chief of the C.I.D.; and Lt.-Colonel James Lunt of the 2nd Armoured Car Regiment, assembled in Hutton's office.

It was decided that such troops as remained in Amman were to be placed under my command. These were the staff, students and recruits of the A.L.T.C., whom Colonel Walden was forming into companies for the time being. These were to guard vulnerable points and embassies, so as to release 9 Regiment as a striking force. The guards at Zerqa were taken over by various base units, and Support Company and H.Q. from Khaw concentrated in the Arab Legion Air Force camp at Merka. There was no proper accommodation for them, but they bivouacked in half-finished buildings, and made the best of it.

The King was due to arrive during the night at Ramthe on the Syrian border, and elaborate precautions were to be taken to safeguard his route to Amman via Zerqa. Twelve armoured cars, which were to report at our Camp at Khaw at 2.30 p.m., were to picket the route, while a force under Salameh Etayek was to search every culvert and to patrol the road until His Majesty had passed, which would be between three and four in the morning.

By seven o'clock next morning I was back at Merka. Salameh arrived and reported that His Majesty had reached Amman safely. After inspecting the force at Merka I moved down to the main Police Station taking with me as a tactical H.Q., Saoud Rashdan; Abdel Rahman Suiss, one of the clerks; Faleh Soud, the sniper and another soldier. Juma'a was driving the Land-Rover, and Awwad Ahmed, the Humber. It was now eight-thirty.

I called on the Chief of Police, Nadeem Saman, who had just returned from greeting the King at Ramthe. We drank coffee. After a short time it was reported that a row had started at King Hussein College, and Nadeem Bey went off to see what was happening. Meanwhile Walden's men were moving down to take over at the various embassies, and by ten o'clock they were all in position.

At ten twenty-eight a message came through from Irbid to say that there was going to be a strike there.

About 11.25 a large procession headed by the girls of Queen Zein School marched down from the Jebel Amman, passed Qiada and demonstrated outside the Prime Minister's office. As soon as this began all the Police officers rushed off leaving me to my own devices. They left no duty officer, and they passed back no information, but at 12.30 Jim Hutton rang up and told me to send thirty men to the Salt road to help the police to disperse the crowd. It was not clear what the crowd wanted — it seldom is — but they felt that the Legion was not sufficiently firm with the Israelis for it was thought that the British officers restrained the soldiers.

Since there was no other way of discovering what was going on I left the Police Headquarters and drove in the Land-Rover up Feisal Street past the Ottoman Bank. By this time the mob was outside Tewfik Abul Huda's office. I left my Land-Rover and walked into one of the Government offices opposite; all the employees were on the balconies watching, and listening to the speeches. I joined them. They did not seem particularly pleased to see me, and one or two people in the street threw things at the window. A small dark girl in a black dress with a ridiculous plastic Eton collar was reading a speech in uninspiring tones. There was a row of police with spiked helmets, perhaps a dozen strong standing in front of the Prime Minister's offices. The crowd did not seem very dangerous, and nobody resisted when two policemen dashed in and seized some young agitator who shouted "Death to Glubb Pasha!" Struggling and resisting he was bundled into the back of an eight hundredweight van; as it drove off the policemen were beating him and cuffing him with their fists; he crouched with his hands over his head to avoid their blows.

I walked down the stairs and out into the sunshine. On the pavement I met Major Muhamad Suheimat, Sir Patrick Coghill's assistant. He asked me to go away, because he was afraid that the crowd was anti-British. I drove back to Police Headquarters, and reported the incident to Jim Hutton on the telephone, mentioning at the same time that there were no police officers in their headquarters. He told me that stones had been thrown at the French embassy, and some of the windows had been broken.

At 12.55 Salameh reported that a platoon had duly joined forces with the police, and I sent him off to find out where the crowd had got to, or whether it had dispersed. Five minutes later it was reported to have gone back up the hill past Qiada without causing any trouble. Three arrests were made.

A quarter of an hour later I had a telephone conversation with Colonel Walden and was told that Ahmed Sudqi Pasha, the second-in-command of the Legion, had ordered out his reserve company without informing me. By this time all was quiet again, the demonstrators presumably having gone off to lunch. Nadeem returned to his office in triumph.

At about 3.30 in the afternoon the boys of the College on Jebel Hussein, not wishing to be outdone by the schoolgirls came marching down the hill towards Feisal Street. A police officer fired his pistol in the air to turn them back, a stupid thing to do, for as soon as he had emptied all six chambers they continued their advance. The shops shut. Once more the police officers rushed out into the streets, but this time it did not matter much as one could see what was going on from the windows of the Police building.

By four o'clock there were some five thousand people demonstrating outside the government offices, and a small crowd had assembled at the police headquarters. Saoud, who had been on his rounds, returned to report that the various police posts had been reinforced by soldiers, and that No. 1 Company was patrolling Feisal Street. Jezzah Ibrahim's platoon arrived at the Police H.Q. and took up positions on the flat roof, which commands a good view of Feisal Street and the Madaba Sûq.

About 4.15 Colonel Walden reported that Ahmed Sudqi Pasha had again intervened, ordering him to put a hundred men under Nadeem Bey's orders to control the Sûq. Quite apart from the fact that these orders should have been given through me, it was obvious that a regular company was more suitable for this task than an ad hoc one, and as it happened a company was already on the job.

By 4.20 the demonstration at Talal Street had ended. Colonel Hutton now told me that Glubb Pasha wanted two companies to drive through the streets to the Parliament House, in order to show the people that we had still got a few reserves up our sleeve: a flag march in fact. Another company was to come to the Police H.Q. I sent Saoud off to brief Salameh.

A few minutes later a soldier on guard at Police H.Q. was hit by stones. The crowd on Feisal Street had been swelling all the time and at about 4.40 there was a big demonstration at the junction of Feisal Street and the Salt road. My two companies were due to arrive there at any moment. I told Abdel Rahman Suiss to run through the streets and intercept Salameh. He was to tell him of this demonstration, give him my orders to contact the police officer there, and ask him whether he wanted them to break up the crowd by force. Abdel Rahman met the convoy near the Philadelphia Hotel and passed my message, and so at 4.55 the mob outside the Ottoman Bank found itself confronted by two companies of bedouin, their shemaghs wrapped over their faces and their bayonets fixed. Three of the less nimble soldiers were hit by stones, and removed to hospital but there was no shooting and towards evening the crowd got tired and dispersed. When from the Police Headquarters we saw the shops beginning to reopen we knew that the trouble was over.

At 5.30 Salameh came into Police H.Q. and reported. The commanders of the armoured cars rang up, and we sent them home. No. 1 Company had suffered a few minor casualties, but there had been no shooting. I reported all this to Colonel Hutton, who approved of our measures, and said he hoped to call later. A little later he rang up to say that the Pasha was going up to the Palace, and to ask what might be the best route for him to take. Ahmed Qasim rang up the Jebel Hussein Police Station and found out that there was no trouble on the back road to the Palace. A little later Sir Patrick Coghill arrived and went off with Saoud and Jezzah to reconnoitre the Pasha's route.

Salameh returned. He had 2 Company in position near the Roman amphitheatre and 3 Company near the chief mosque. I sent him with a platoon to patrol the danger point on the Pasha's route, which I took to be the road junctions at the top of Feisal Street. All these precautions were unnecessary for by 6.45 when Sir Patrick returned the Sûq was empty. We were joined by Jim Hutton, who said that there had been thirty-three arrests so far.

That night I slept in Police H.Q.

I awoke early and at six a.m. sent Abdel Rahman in my Land-Rover to see whether the platoon from 3 Company had arrived at the Prime Minister's office. It had. At about seven while I was driving around, I met a company coming down into the town from the A.L.T.C.: this time the Chief of Police had been giving orders. I sent them back and went to see Nadeem Bey.

The morning passed peacefully until 12.10 when it was reported that there was a row going on in the Hussein College. We rang up the local police station, and it transpired that the trouble was confined to the schoolyard. By 12.30 it was all over.

The following day was Friday, and it was thought possible that there would be trouble when the people dispersed from the Mosques after prayer. There was not. The Qibya riots were over.

Miles Pulford and 1 Regiment were ordered back from Palestine to assist us, but they were not deployed. In those days bedouin regiments were always used in aid to the civil power as they were considered to be more reliable than the haderi regiments.

After the Qibya incident the Legion took some time to return to normal; the garrison of the West Bank, hitherto only one brigade, was doubled; 1 Brigade taking over Nablus and 2 Brigade, Jerusalem. 3 Brigade, which had spent so long in

Palestine, came to Khaw and Brigadier Ashton returned to England. It was felt by the British officers that he had been made a scapegoat, and that if anyone was to blame it was not he. However, there was not much we could do about it, since there was no clause in the Treaty to say that the Jordanians must retain whatever officers the British army cared to send them. Kamel Abdel Kader was sent into retirement, but he emerged a few weeks later, and was given some job in the recruiting line, which did not call for much tactical knowledge.

Meanwhile 9 Regiment remained in splendid isolation. Brigade H.Q. had gone away and, as I have mentioned earlier, we came directly under Qiada, where I had a good "fifth column". It was a wonderful opportunity to make up all our deficiencies in weapons and vehicles, and the Regiment lacked nothing. And there was no need to submit training programmes. We still had to perform our guard duties, but we were able to put in some valuable weapon training for at this time Captain Keith O'Kelly, a small arms expert from the Parachute Brigade in the Canal Zone, came to run pistol and sten courses for the Legion. It chanced that I had met this officer in Egypt, and he readily agreed to instruct a special class from 9 Regiment, which assembled each afternoon. In this way we built up a body of really first-class instructors, two or three from each company. I was vain enough to suppose that I was a deadly shot with a pistol, but I had always been brought up to fire with a straight arm. O'Kelly soon proved to me that I knew nothing. In close-quarter fighting seconds count, and "the battle crouch" is the thing! We were taught to shoot from the hip, and were amazed to find that by pointing the barrel as if it was one's right forefinger you really could put a couple of bullets in the target's stomach. The old duelling pistol style of marksman would be dead and gone before he had time to take aim at O'Kelly!

I had never thought much of the sten as a weapon, and indeed its manufacture leaves something to be desired, but we soon had a lot of confident operators, able to shoot accurately at fifty yards range, hit tins while firing from the hip, and keep them moving at twenty or thirty yards. Bob Young came out and took pictures, and a pamphlet was written and translated for the use of the whole Legion.

Annual confidential reports were written for every officer, N.C.O. and man, and were secret. Officers were not required to initial their reports, but even so Arab C.O.s whether because they are too kind-hearted, or because they are afraid that their remarks will come to light and be held against them, are extremely reluctant to describe the failings of their followers. For this reason a five-or six-page document, in both languages, was devised, which listed every known military virtue and defect. At the top of each page were written: Excellent, Good, Fair, Bad, and Nil. All the C.O. had to do was to put an X in the appropriate column. If you thought that a man's belief in the value of prayer was Nil you merely put an X in the space provided. It was made perfectly clear by elaborate notes that if a man was notoriously keen on sexual offences the X was not meant to go under Excellent.

Other ranks had a less elaborate report, but even these I found I had to attend to myself, as a company commander was quite capable of recommending that a man should be promoted according to his seniority, when from the rest of his report it appeared that he was idle, inefficient, and illiterate. Qiada took great note of these reports and it is true to say that no man could be promoted without his C.O.'s recommendation. It is equally true to say that many of those whom C.O.s would like to have seen promoted were held back, either because the higher ranks were already full up to establishment, or because their past crimes were better known in Qiada than in the regiments.

It was not until 12th November, that we were finally relieved from guard duties. About this time I learned from General Cooke that we would be going to Jerusalem early in the following February to rejoin our own brigade.

Brigadier Parry had now arrived from Egypt and taken command of 3 Brigade. He was responsible for the instruction of a National Guard battalion which had been called up for training at Khaw. 9 Regiment had to give a number of demonstrations, which were useful training for our men. Khdayer Qa'aid the anti-tank platoon commander, who had been at Eaton Hall, proved to have a flair for this work, while Sukheil Hammad, a solid Iraqi with a big black moustache, at least proved that he had remembered various drills he had been taught during the summer.

Walter Skrine, who had been in Sicily with 3 Commando, spent the winter with us. Before he left we determined to visit Azrak, and see the castle which was Lawrence's Headquarters in 1917-18. On the way we saw a fox and I explained to Juma'a as best I could the way foxes are hunted in England. The castle stands in a Druze village, flanked to the East by palm trees, some of which Lawrence's men had cut down and used to support the roofs of the rooms they made habitable. Some of the beams they made are still in position. We had lunch in the old fortress, took some photos, and then went to look for duck. We merely succeeded in getting wet. On the way home we saw another fox, this time in our headlights. Juma'a, fired by our conversation during the morning, without so much as a "By your leave", shot after it. The fox dodged about here and there, the Land-Rover bumped across the desert in pursuit. Tigla, deeply interested, stood on the seat behind me, her nose on my right shoulder, looking out of the foot-square opening in the window. The fox was not far ahead, when suddenly the old girl shot over my shoulder and out of the window, landed like a cat, and took up the chase on her own account!

During the last weeks at Khaw we acted as enemy for two of a series of exercises carried out near Mafraq by the Parachute Brigade from the Canal Zone. The parachutists were attacking. The bedouin have one great virtue uncommon among British soldiers. They keep still. Their positions are not betrayed by unnecessary movement. In exercises Lionheart I and II they managed to hold their own: they dug in well, sited reasonable positions, and when they had to move they went fast.

I was looking forward to taking them to Jerusalem, confident that they would not blacken my face when we got there.

CHAPTER IV: UNEASY FRONTIER

In February 1954, we moved to Jerusalem and rejoined 2 Brigade, taking over from 4 Regiment in the Old City area. This was a haderi battalion, commanded by Major Mahmoud Moussa, who as a company commander had won a Gallantry Medal in the fighting in Jerusalem in 1948. He spoke very little English and was reputedly anti-British. I was always on friendly terms with him, although he failed to give satisfaction to a succession of British brigadiers, and eventually found himself promoted and removed to the command of the National Guard at Nablus. I can only say that 4 Regiment feasted our officers, gave us a good hand-over, and last but not least found me a house!

2 Brigade had altered the inter-regimental boundaries and so I took over part of my area from Lt.-Col. Fawwaz Maher, whom I also found friendly and helpful. Fawwaz, who is a Circassian, now commands 2 Brigade and is one of the senior officers of the Arab Legion. He is big and blond, well over six foot, and would pass as an Englishman or a German. He also won the Gallantry Medal in 1948. He took me round his part of the front line, showing me in detail the defence work that was going forward, and explaining his plans with obvious enthusiasm. He would stand on the flat roof of a house pointing out the Israeli posts forty or fifty yards away and analysing their arrangements with the utmost confidence and in fluent English. I was impressed.

I imagine that most of the British officers preferred serving on the West Bank rather than the East. In the first place the climate in the Judean hills is delightful, even at midsummer, for

Jerusalem stands 2,550 feet above sea level. At Zerqa our time was spent in training, doing guard duties, guards of honour and so forth. All very well in its way, but not to be compared with the active life that a regiment leads in the border zone, with the chance of an incident ever present, and the knowledge that the Israelis are always on the lookout for the unwary.

9 Regiment as a body had never been on the West Bank before, although there were still over a hundred officers and soldiers who had fought there in 1948. In Jerusalem we normally had two rifle companies in the front-line, and two in reserve, where they could carry on with their normal training, though they had to provide patrols and ambushes at night. The companies in the forward area spent their days improving the defence works.

On the afternoon that we arrived I was visiting one of my companies, when the Brigadier rang up and told me that he was leaving for England next day as his father was dangerously ill. And so for the first fortnight of our stay in Jerusalem I found myself commanding not only the Regiment, but the Brigade, whose front ran, roughly speaking, from Ramallah to Hebron. Lt.-Col. Izzat Hassan, the Circassian commander of 6 Regiment, had had the southern sector for several months and already knew it well. To my North was Fawwaz Maher with 5 Regiment.

Although the men had carried out countless exercises where they had to dig in in the open field, usually in the desert, they had no previous experience of the defence of a built-up area. To the bedouin, accustomed to living in tents in the back of beyond, it was a strange experience to find themselves in the Citadel of Jerusalem or in a house in the Musrara. Moreover, many of the posts were unfinished, and although the Legion had been in them for five years the living accommodation was very haphazard. Men were sleeping in twos and threes in sandbagged rooms in between the defence posts.

In the Old City the position was much better. There was plenty of room in the towers and in the Citadel to quarter the men in comparative comfort. The defence problem was straightforward, for it was largely a matter of manning the ancient city walls and the flanking towers. A little old-fashioned perhaps, but the walls are thick and strong, and in 1948 they had survived practically unscathed, when many of the modern buildings were reduced to rubble.

The walls of Jerusalem as they stand today were built or rather restored by Suleiman the Magnificent between 1536 and 1539, as is recorded in various commemorative inscriptions on the gates and at other points on them. The walls vary in height and thickness, being strongest where the ground favours an attacker, and they enclose an irregular quadrilateral. Sections of the wall on the North and West are hidden by ugly modern houses, which the Turks allowed to be built during the latter years of their regime. There are eleven gates of which the finest is the Damascus Gate, known to the Arabs as the Bab el 'Amud, or Gate of the Pillar. This, the main entrance from the North, is quite different from any of the others, and is flanked by two strong machicolated towers.

Walking eastwards you come next to Herod's Gate, the Bab ez Zahira, near which time out of mind the sheep market has been held. The only open gate on the East wall is St. Stephen's, the Bab Sittna Maryam, the link between the Old City and Mary's Well by the garden of Gethsemane. The beautiful Golden Gate is closed, awaiting the second coming of Our Lord. The Dung Gate in the South Wall is remarkable only because in recent times a road has been constructed, which enters the City, here and, running along inside the wall, passes through the Armenian quarter to the Citadel.

The Zion Gate, known locally as the Bab en Nebi Daoud, is in the Southern wall about two hundred yards from the South West corner. It has been blocked up solid with masonry since 1948, for not a hundred yards away on Mount Zion the Church of the Dormition is held by the Israelis. This was a staggered gate involving a right wheel to enter the City, and above it is a strong tower with fine windows and machicolis.

To the West the Jaffa Gate, known to the Arabs as the Bab el Khalil or Hebron Gate, is also built up, and so is the breach made between it and the Citadel in 1898, for the triumphal entry on horseback of Kaiser Wilhelm I. In 1917 Allenby entered here on foot. Outside against the wall ugly two-storeyed houses, which marred its appearance in Mandate days, have been smashed beyond repair in the 1948 fighting. The Jaffa Gate projects from the wall, and though blocked up at present still does duty as a tower. The New Gate, made in 1889, was simply a breach in the wall made to give access to the Christian Quarter of the Old City. It is now walled up again, for the Notre Dame de France, an Israeli fortress, is not fifty yards away.

In 1917 the Turks were driven from the City. Had one of the delivering army then prophesied that in 1954 the bedouin of the desert would man its towers, he would have been thought a poor prophet indeed.

Since the New Gate and the Zion Gate had been built up with masonry, there was now no entrance between the Damascus Gate and the Dung Gate, except for an iron postern in the Jaffa Gate, which was opened at Easter for members of the Diplomatic Corps. Brigadier Green and I considered this was a wholly unnecessary risk, and we had it walled up on the inside, much to the annoyance of the diplomats, who had now to go round by the Mandelbaum Gate. The strength of the Old City was such that we decided to reduce the garrison and increase our reserves.

The Mandelbaum Gate in the Musrara quarter is the authorized crossing point between Jordan and Israel. It is used by the diplomatic corps, United Nations Officers, and such travellers as have two passports, for no Arab country will accept a visitor who has an Israeli visa. A hundred yards apart stand two huts at the side of a street. These are the Jordanian and Israeli police posts, which with a few dragon's teeth in the road represent the Mandelbaum Gate. At night a portable barricade is put across the road and the gate is closed. It seems that one Mandelbaum formerly owned an apartment house at this place, and there has never been any actual gate.

The Citadel, which as good fortune would have it, stands on the West, the side exposed to the Israelis, dates from the fourteenth century. There was a Crusader castle on the site in the twelfth century, but the present fortress was built by the Moslem rulers of Egypt after they had driven the crusaders from Acre. There is evidence of much older work. To the right, (North) as you enter, stands the Tower of David, which is one of the three built by Herod the Great after he captured Jerusalem in 37 B.C. This, the tower named Phasael, was 140 feet high and was solid to nearly half its height. It has great courses ten feet long and four feet thick, like those of the Wailing Wall, which dates from the same period. When Titus took and destroyed Jerusalem in A.D. 70, he did not destroy Herod's three great square towers, but turned the palace into barracks for the Roman garrison. During the excavations in the Citadel, a drain was found made up of pottery pipes with the stamp of the Tenth Legion; one of those which went with Julius Caesar to Britain.

Formerly the Old City of Jerusalem was divided into four "quarters", Christian, Moslem, Armenian and Jewish. During the fighting in 1948 the Jews were forced to surrender, and the houses that survived in their quarter are now inhabited by Arab refugees.

The fighting did little to impair the beauty of the Old City. The tourist or pilgrim, with limited time at his disposal, who visits the religious sites and historic buildings, has hardly time to see the things that delight one who daily walks the walls, or wanders through the stone paved Sûq: the domed roofs and the minarets; high saracen arches; vaulted passages; the shady courtyards with their arcades, their trellised vines and their cypress trees; the carved and latticed oriels high above narrow streets.

Well behind the Arab lines to the East of the City lies the Mount Scopus ridge, the southern end of which is the Mount of Olives. It is not too much to say that this ridge, from which one can see the Dead Sea and the Mountains of Moab, dominates the City. It was here that Saladin placed his besieging army when he took Jerusalem in 1187. A great part of this ridge is in Jewish hands as a result of an unfortunate and ill-considered armistice agreement made in 1948. This enclave includes the Hebrew University and the Hadassah Hospital, which are garrisoned by rather more than one hundred Israeli policemen, armed with small arms and light machine-guns, but, at least in theory, with no heavy weapons. This garrison is supplied by a fortnightly convoy which, searched and supervised by United Nations Officers, passes in blacked-out buses through the Mandelbaum Gate. Perhaps one third of the personnel at the Hadassah are changed each fortnight. Theoretically the area is unfortified, but in fact I often saw the garrison toiling at its defences, and our intelligence section spent happy hours watching the sentries on the Amphitheatre of the Hebrew University, and plotting enemy positions, real and imaginary. One could see with the naked eye how trees had been lopped and boundary walls lowered to clear fields of fire.

The garrison of the Hadassah were reputedly somewhat trigger-happy, and never a week went by without a few shots being reported from their direction. Perhaps being so far behind our lines they used to see the trees advancing towards them at night.

Working on the defences of Jerusalem was intensely interesting. When the fighting had ended six years before, the Legion was strongly posted in the houses of the Musrara and northern suburbs. Here during the course of time the opposing forces had settled down with a No Man's Land of varying width between them. The line followed the Nablus road lying parallel to it and a little further West. The regiments who had held Jerusalem since 1948 had worked at the defences with varying degrees of ardour. One C.O. had been a great tunneller, another had made ramps so that Land-Rovers could reach the Citadel, up the streets in the Old City; others had preferred to rest on their laurels.

In the last war and particularly in Normandy I had seen a fair variety of field-works, both British and German, and the bedouin now had the opportunity of learning this new art in the most practical way, by constructing their own positions.

The first thing was to check the soundness or otherwise of the existing defensive arrangements. The front line was not, of course, continuous and it was clearly important that each post should be sited for all-round defence in case the enemy should pass between them under cover of night or smoke. Most of the posts had reasonable fields of fire to their front and their flanks, but were not defended from the rear. Our first task was to overcome this danger, and occasionally this meant taking over and fortifying buildings occupied by civilians. At places it seemed to me that the intervals between our posts were too great, and could not be covered by fire. This again was overcome by occupying houses or gardens, which had been abandoned at the end of hostilities. Never a fortnight went by without a visit from Glubb Pasha, and he gave us every encouragement by acquiring such sites as were necessary to complete our dispositions.

Meanwhile walls were erected to screen the Nablus road in the Wadi Joz, by the American Consulate, and at the Damascus Gate. These were loopholed, but their chief purpose was to protect vehicles and passers-by from indiscriminate shooting. At one point we re-opened a section of the Roman road to Ramallah, in order to by-pass a dangerous corner in the Sheikh Jerrah quarter.

In most of our positions the windows and doors facing towards Israel were blocked up with sandbags. These had been filled with earth in 1948 and had long since burst, so we gradually replaced them all with masonry. Abu Mudhish, who commanded one of the forward companies, became an expert at siting loopholes, seeing that the builders defiladed them and did not make them too large; but I enjoyed doing this work myself, and scarcely a day went by that I did not tour the Musrara and the Old City walls. If I was lucky I got in two visits and was able to see how much progress the men had made in the day.

The accommodation also needed attention. Many of the houses had two or three storeys, and since after all this was only a cold war we made it a matter of general policy to turn the upper storeys into barrack-rooms, and the lower into defensive positions. It was a simple matter for the soldiers to run downstairs in case of an alarm; and their beds and boxes no longer cluttered up the defences. In one case the stairs to the second storey were outside the house on the side facing the Israelis, and in consequence nobody had been upstairs since the war. The upper floor was filled with inflammable debris of every sort, until an iron ladder was installed and it was cleared. Another problem which demanded attention was the provision of covered approaches to each post, a point which had been much neglected in the past.

After a few weeks the men got into the swing of this work, and its progress came to depend not so much on their diligence as on the supply of cement from Brigade, and the energy of the attached Sapper officer. By far the most industrious of these was a Captain called Ahmed Zarour, who has now risen to be the C.O. of the Engineer Regiment.

Far be it from me to give more than the vaguest indications of the defence works which 9 Regiment constructed in Jerusalem; they occupied most of my waking hours for many months, and were fairly well advanced before the Israelis took it into their heads to shoot at us. *El Hamdulillah!*

By March the Regiment had settled down in Jerusalem, all was quiet and more than half the officers were away on courses.

Salameh was in England, and the other captains had either left or were about to. Muhamad Mohsin was in the National Guard and Abu Ghazi was going to the Main Stores.

Khdayer Qa'aid, from the 6-pounder platoon, took over Support Company, and Saleem Qurani became Quartermaster, while Farhan Abdel Mahdi, who has always done all the work in any case, became R.Q.M.S. The Quartermaster, Rais Abdul Rahman Mustafa, was of course a haderi. He was a quiet, pale, mild-mannered man, who spent long hours in his office working, not at his ledgers, but for his promotion exam. After the clothing exchange in 1952 he had been court-martialled, but had survived to receive the Istiqlal (Fourth Class). His assistant the R.Q.M.S. was an insolent and sinister-looking waqil called Mahmoud Sadiq. Both were content to permit Farhan Abdel Mahdi to do their work, and in this they were quite right, for he understood it much better than they did. Mahmoud Sadiq, who had long had his eye on Abu Ghazi's chair, had misplayed his hand, not knowing my plans for Abu Ghazi's future, and contrived to get himself a job in the police about a fortnight earlier. Had he remained I might have had to accept him as Quartermaster.

At the beginning of April Glubb Pasha sent me the results of the officers' promotion examination, which were very satisfactory. Seven out of nine had passed, though Waqil Abdulla Dahil managed to fail in all subjects; and Muhamad Moazi was defeated by military law and administration, which, however, he managed to pass the following July. Musayeb Suleiman, Dghayem Ghazi, Khdayer Qa'aid, Mansour Kreishan, Shayem Oudeh, Muhamad Rkheimeh, Bedr Mansour and Jezzah Ibrahim all passed, but two of them, lacking my recommendation, were not promoted. The one too dearly loved the bottle, and the other had failed to distinguish himself in the fighting at Latroun in 1948.

A few weeks later we received our 17-pounder platoon, which came as a body from the 4th Artillery Regiment. The G.O., Keith Edison, wrote that when officers were being selected to go from anti-tank batteries to infantry battalions, Second Lieutenant Mseifer Murki had asked to go to 9

Regiment. Keith said that this officer was aged about thirty, was cheerful and industrious and ran a good troop, all of which was perfectly true. He was welcome, for by a little unofficial selection he had brought a grand lot of men with him, all with between three and four years' service, and including a number of potential N.C.O.s. He had selected them himself, so he said, and according to their former C.O. we were getting the pick of the bunch. Mseifer rose to command Support Company. There were some good men in the old 6-pounder platoon and a number of these remained anti-tank gunners. At the same time one of the battery commanders, Suwwan Bikheitan, a senior lieutenant, was transferred to the Regiment. A Jebel bedouin, with a sound knowledge of English, he suffered from the delusion that he ought upon arrival to be made Adjutant.

On 27th April we drove over to see the Arab Legion Day Parade which was held for the first time at Khaw, but was on much the same lines as the murassim at Merka the previous year. At the end of the parade His Majesty made a speech in which, after expressing his pride in the Army, he said:

"I thank all those who are engaged in organizing, equipping and training it, for their devoted and successful efforts. In this connection I cannot omit my thanks to our Ally for the valuable assistance which she gives to our Army.

"Ever since I assumed my Constitutional Powers, I have realised that our military situation imposes upon us the duty of constant vigilance and of continual readiness, while at the same time our financial resources are inadequate to meet the duty imposed upon us of defending our country. We have clearly informed our Arab brothers of the true facts of the situation. They joined us in meeting some of the expenses of the National Guard. We offer them our deepest thanks for their assistance and we wish once more to proclaim clearly that the

Palestine Case is a problem affecting all the Arabs and indeed all the Islamic World."

Early in May we were visited by a party from the Canadian National Defence College, at Fort Frontenac, Kingston, Ontario. We took them up to Et Tur, whence from the roof of a mosque on the summit of the Mount of Olives we could survey the panorama of Jerusalem laid out before us. To our right stood the Augusta Victoria, which stands in neutral ground; further along Mount Scopus some of the buildings of the Hebrew University in the Israeli enclave were visible. Beyond, but out of sight, lay French Hill then held by io Regiment.

Far away to the West we could see Nebi Samwil, the place from which Coeur de Lion had his only glimpse of the Holy City and the key to Jerusalem in the 1917 fighting. Then the Sheikh Jerrah suburb to the North of the Wadi Joz; St. George's Cathedral, with its tower like an English country church, standing just inside Jordan, and the Italian Hospital whose narrow tower now forms an Israeli observation post; the Notre Dame with the great breach battered in its East wall by the guns of the Arab Legion, and nearer the earthquake-proof Museum, founded by one of the Rockefellers. The Old City with the Dome of the Rock standing alone and beautiful in the great enclosure of the Haram es Sharif, its delicate mosaics still scarred by Israeli mortar bombs; then the Mosque el Aqsa, the Far Mosque. It was in the doorway of this building that King Abdulla was murdered in 1951. In the midst of the City the white pointed tower of the Lutheran church stands up, with the two domes, one white and one black, of the Church of the Holy Sepulchre a little to its right. The great square yellowish towers of the Citadel, easily seen in the morning light, and beyond the tall plain rather ugly tower of the Y.M.C.A. over in the Western suburbs where the Israelis have made their capital. The South wall of the Old City zigzags down from Mount Zion towards the Far Mosque and over against it is the Church of the Dormition with its Israeli garrison. To the South on the tree-crowned summit of Deir Abu Tor is another Israeli post; while far away behind on the far horizon stands Government House, now neutral and the headquarters of the United Nations Observers, and a little nearer, beside the Brook Kedron, Silwan village, the ancient Siloam, stands on the steep hillside, a natural fortress.

Turning round and looking Eastwards into the sun, far below we could see the Dead Sea, blue and hazy in the heat. In the foreground are Bethany and Abu Dis. The mosque, which affords such a perfect view, stands at the place of the Ascension.

Afterwards we visited the Citadel to take from the roof of Phasael a nearer view of the neighbours, and the No Man's Land. On this very roof in 1948 some enterprising warrior — allegedly a British warrant officer — got a 6-pounder gun into action against the Israelis in the King David Hotel. The top of the tower is well spattered and pock-marked with bullet holes. The inevitable tea-party followed in the courtyard, and with much mirth those of the bedouin officers who spoke any English tried it on the visitors. Then we all drove up to French Hill, and Suleiman Masoud, the Major commanding 10 Regiment, pointed out how the land lay on his side.

We frequently had to arrange conducted tours of this sort, for no officer who visited Jordan could leave contented without seeing the Holy City. But most of the visitors were pilgrims pure and simple. Most of the military officers who came had some inkling of the situation on the frontier. Of the more normal travellers few indeed understood that the Holy City was divided. Naib Majid Ibrahim, a quiet-mannered and benevolent youth, who acted as Intelligence Officer at this time, was a zealous spy hunter, ever on the alert to pounce on the unwary pilgrim. One of his first victims was an old Cypriot peasant, grey whiskered, with black baggy trousers and leggings. He had strayed from his friends and after wandering about the Christian quarter trying to get his bearings had climbed on to the Old City wall near the New Gate where some watchful bedouin jundi had apprehended him. I was driving towards St. Stephen's Gate, when I saw a Land-Rover coming towards us. Majid, smiling and happy, sat beside the driver, and Demetrios So-and-So, with an armed escort, sat in the back, his whole head shrouded in a towel. His passport was in order.

Louis Adam, a Parisian, fell into the hands of Abdulla Said, our black M.T. sergeant. He had climbed Mount Scopus one warm day, and taken his shirt off to sunbathe on the hillside near to the Hadassah. Not only was this eccentric Franzawi exposing his body, but he had practically entered the barbed wire of the Israeli enclave. This one I met at the bottom of the Wadi Joz as I was going in the Humber to the Old City. Monsieur Adam had no difficulty in explaining that he was one of a party of pilgrims.

One afternoon I was told on the telephone that another prisoner was languishing in our camp on the Mount of Olives. When I arrived I discovered a Finn, who had a leg in plaster, and walked with the aid of crutches. This villain had aroused Majid's suspicions by painting landscapes.

But Majid's great feat was the capture of Don Candido Bengoa, a worthy Spanish priest and chaplain to a vessel named the *Cabo de Homos*, who had achieved a lifetime's ambition by coming from Bilbao to see the Holy Places. The bedouin spotted him running with pious zeal towards the pool of Siloam, and had no doubt that he was attempting to infiltrate into Israel. This view had been further confirmed by an inspection of his documents and the discovery of his name — Bengoa sounded to them altogether too like Ben Gurion.

I returned home that evening to find a curious party in my dining-room: Ahmed Qasim, wearing his greatcoat over his pyjamas, Majid, Don Candido and an Arab, who, having lived in Nicaragua and being able to speak some form of Spanish, was acting as interpreter. Joan was treating the Don for shock with draughts of brandy.

The road to our house was shattering enough at the best of times, but Majid, following his usual custom, had blindfolded his victim before putting him in the Land-Rover. Don Candido, doubtless with memories of the Civil War in the back of his mind, thought his last hour was come, and was still in a state of considerable perturbation when I arrived. We conversed in indifferent French, and as he sat talking he fidgeted about so much that his beret kept falling off his knee on to the floor. When I told him that I proposed to release him he looked about saying, "Je suis libre? Je suis libre?" in incredulous tones. Don Candido has remembered his liberator every Christmas, with a card saying that he will never forget his adventure.

Majid, who came from Irbid district, left at the end of the year for the Cadet School, and thereafter our bag of prisoners dwindled. If he was sometimes a trifle over-zealous in this matter, I did not care to discourage him. At least he had initiative.

During our first few months in the line we had only one incident worthy of a complaint. One night a sentry near the entrance to one of our posts in the Musrara quarter was fired at by an Israeli patrol, which stalked through No Man's Land and entered a row of empty and derelict houses just beyond the wire in the Street of the Prophets. A burst of fire, apparently from a sten, hit the wall just above the sentry, who, like an idiot, was standing in the moonlight instead of lurking in the shadows. The other sentry, Fankhour Mite'b, a Jebeli bedu, was manning a bren gun on top of a sort of tower, which formed part of the post. He replied to the fire with a burst from the bren, and the post stood to. The Israeli patrol made off, and that was all there was to it. I went there at once, but by the time I arrived everything was as silent as the grave. I stayed on the roof for a time, but there was no movement to be seen either in No Man's Land or the Israeli posts, the nearest of which was only about thirty yards away — so near indeed that the Jews sometimes used to throw stones at the house we occupied in the hope that the soldiers would fire back and give them grounds for a complaint.

When there was an incident of this sort, Brigade would report it to the officer representing Jordan on the Mixed Armistice Committee, who would submit a complaint to the United Nations Headquarters.

Commander Hutchinson, U.S. Navy, was Chairman of the Mixed Armistice Commission nearly all the time I was at Jerusalem. The Arabs had great confidence in this officer, who was known to be scrupulously impartial. Any frontier incident was investigated by his team of United Nations Observers, who included Canadian, New Zealand, American, French, Swedish and Danish officers. Their findings were discussed by the Mixed Armistice Commission, whose members were two Jordanians, two Israelis and Hutch. Whatever the evidence, the Israelis and the Jordanians naturally voted for their own side, and so the full burden of deciding whether one side or the other was to be condemned fell upon the Chairman. The Israelis had walked out of the M.A.C. some months before I reached Jerusalem, being dissatisfied with Hutch's decision in the Scorpion's Pass incident.[5]

A more serious incident happened early in June, when the Brigadier was away. I was told that there had been shooting at Wadi Foukine in Izzat Hassan's area, and I hastened there to find out what was going on. The village itself was quiet as we drove up, but a long rocky ridge to the South-East was alive with people. There were soldiers from 6 Regiment, men of the police cavalry and National Guardsmen crouching behind boulders, perhaps sixty in all. None of the villagers was in uniform, though all were armed. One old man, who must have been seventy and had hardly a tooth in his head, told me that his son had been killed by the Israelis and so it fell to him in his old age to shoulder a rifle.

I found Izzat Hassan and Commander Hutchinson, who told me that a patrol of Israelis had crossed the frontier, which was not at all clearly demarcated at this point, and were coming down a forward slope when one of Izzat's Observation Posts had opened fire on them, killing three. One man, who was thought to have been wounded, had run back over the skyline. At least one of Izzat's men had a rifle with a telescopic sight. After this incident Israeli troops had manned the hills on their side of the line and opened fire. One woman in the village was wounded by a stray shot.

According to one of the United Nations officers, who had come to the incident from the Israel side, the Jewish soldiers

---

[5] In 1953 a bus had been ambushed. No proof existed that Jordanians were responsible, but the Israelis were indignant that Jordan had not been condemned.

were so incensed that one of them had tried to attack him, and had only been restrained by an officer.

Hutch was in wireless touch with his observers on the other side, and after a time was told that the Israelis wanted to carry out investigations on our side of the line. I immediately said that there was no objection from our point of view, and that I would ensure that they were not fired upon. Five minutes later we received another message saying that they no longer wanted to come. Perhaps they had expected that their original request would be refused, and that they would be able to complain that we had obstructed the investigation.

That night I saw the bodies of the Israeli soldiers handed over at the Mandelbaum Gate. There was no demonstration, merely a sad little group of the men's relations waiting at the crossroads beyond the dragon's teeth.

From August to December another British officer served in the Regiment: his name was John Adair, a National Service Ensign from the battalion of the Scots Guards then stationed in the Canal Zone, and he contrived to get himself attached to the Legion. Before he arrived the Brigadier asked how I proposed to employ this officer, for he was all in favour of attached officers having a job to do. I said that I thought of making him my Adjutant, as he would then see more of what went on, and so get to know more about the Legion. The Brigadier thought this might not work, as the existing staff of the Regiment might be offended, but he left it to me.

At this period my bedouin adjutant, newly appointed, was an Iraqi subaltern, Khdayer Qa'aid, who had joined the Jeish as a boy of about fifteen, and had served in 1 Regiment and later in the Pasha's bodyguard. He had been a cadet at Eaton Hall and spoke English well. I had no doubt that Saoud Rashdan and Khdayer would make Adair welcome, and in this I was not

deceived. I merely mentioned to Saoud that a Mulazim Thani
from the Jeish el Inglezi was coming to be attached and asked
him to set a room aside for the guest. Haj Ibrhim was available
to act as his batman. I had found him too talkative and had
recently replaced him by a Palestinian, Ali, the regimental
gardener, who proved an excellent and loyal servant. He was
dead lame from a wound received when as a boy he had served
with the Iraqi army in 1948. Unfortunately when we went back
to Khaw I had to let him return to the Regiment, otherwise the
trees in the camp would have been allowed to die for lack of
water.

When John Adair arrived he was taken to the Mess by Saoud
Rashdan and introduced to some of the officers. Khdayer took
the Arabic stars off his own battledress and gave them to
Adair, sending at the same time for a shemagh and agal for
him. Soon the Guards Ensign was transformed into a bedouin
Mulazim Thani, complete with Arab name, for Musayeb could
not pronounce John Adair and dubbed him "Sweillim". The
name stuck. From this moment the officers made much of
Sweillim, who rapidly learned enough Arabic for everyday
purposes and adapted himself to the customs of the bedu. He
had one sharp lesson when, in an unguarded moment, he
admired a loud American tie that Dghayem Ghazi wore with
his civilian clothes, and in the best Arab style was promptly
given it. Sweillim, not to be outdone, took off his own and
presented it to the bibulous Dghayem, a most unsuitable
character to wear the Brigade of Guards tie!

He was invaluable. He ran refresher courses for junior
N.C.O.s, who were assembled in our beautiful new barrack
rooms in the Mandelbaum — and polished until they shone!
He took our athletics team in hand, and they won the brigade
sports, and while I was on leave in Cyprus he kept up a

running commentary on events in the Regiment during my absence. Of these the most important was the winning of the Lash Cup. This is a great silver trophy presented annually to the Regiment whose rifle team gets the highest score in the Legion. Our team had won it in Watson's day, but had lost it in 1953 under circumstances over which a discreet veil should be drawn. Suffice to say that the Hashemite Regiment had been permitted to supply the entire butt party.

Saleem Qurani, the Quartermaster, a steady old officer, and himself a very good shot, had trained the team. This was a great triumph, for the glittering cup was so big and bright that the bedouin were deeply impressed by it. Saoud Rashdan made a great feast and guests came from far and near, including Mithgal Pasha, the great chief of the Beni Sakhr; the Governor of Jerusalem; and the Archimandrite Theodosios.

The latter, who presides over a Greek Orthodox Convent at Bethany, became a great friend of the Regiment during our stay in Jerusalem. At one period some of our vehicles were kept in an olive grove belonging to the Convent, and some of the drivers rented houses belonging to the Convent. It might almost be said that he became Greek Orthodox Padre to the Regiment. He was at Kallandia Airport with the officers when they greeted me on my return from leave. Advancing and seizing me in a bearlike grip, he kissed me in the most determined manner, to the delight of my bedouin followers. Resistance was useless. Theodosios had been present in the Mosque el Aksa on the terrible day when King Abdulla was murdered, and his beard, so he told me, went white that night.

John Adair told me that on the return journey from Khaw after this victory, when they reached the Inn of the Good Samaritan between Jerusalem and Jericho, he had to stop the truck, because the team were sitting in the back letting off their rifles in a continual *feu de joie*! This is a custom among the bedouin in moments of exhilaration. Once, in 1955, when returning from a brigade exercise near Irbid, I was standing beside the road checking up to see whether the drivers were keeping the correct intervals between their vehicles. The soldiers, evidently having acquitted themselves to their own satisfaction, rode past chanting their three-note battle songs and saluting me with volleys of blank cartridges, loosed off into the air! It was a delightful moment. The bedouin can be maddeningly obtuse when he pleases, but he gets away with a lot from sheer charm. John Adair told me that, exasperated at some fiasco, I once said to him: "The bedouin are really only good at being people!" This, needless to say, was a horrible exaggeration, for the best of them can hold their own with any soldiers in the world.

In the autumn elections were held, and engendered a good deal of heat. Rioting was expected in Jerusalem, and I was told to get in touch with the chief of police, Colonel Abdul Haleem Saket. The Arabs seldom make any trouble so long as the authorities are ready for them beforehand, and so we decided to bring down reinforcements on the previous day. We put an extra platoon into the Old City and a company at the Police Headquarters, besides guards outside the various consulates and the Defence Minister's house. I warned the troops in the various platoon positions to be ready to sally forth and reinforce these sentries if necessary. Saoud, Khdayer, Sweillim and I toured the City in our Land-Rovers at frequent intervals so that we would know in good time if trouble was brewing. Since the Jerusalem incident the inhabitants had been well disposed towards the Regiment, and, realising that we were fully occupied in protecting them from the Israelis, they were good enough to get on with their election peaceably.

It was not so everywhere. In Ramallah, for example, road blocks were erected, and a British Information Centre was wrecked. Troops were then called in and a student was shot dead. It was thought that the major in charge of the police was at fault for not asking for the military in time.

At this election the soldiers, including the bedouin, perhaps half of whom were not Jordanian citizens, were permitted to vote. In 9 Regiment most of the men voted for Anwar Nuseibeh, whom they rightly regarded as a friend to the Regiment and to the Jeish. It was reported that thirteen of 2 Brigade Signals Troop voted for the bathis, who are about as extreme as the communists. A fine state of affairs if our communications were in the hands of such unreliable elements. After this election there was a good deal of muttering; some saying that the elections had been rigged.

In November Field-Marshal Sir John Harding, who was then Chief of the Imperial General Staff, came to Jerusalem whilst on a tour of Jordan. The Regiment mounted a Guard of Honour at Kallandia. This was the last event of any note during our first tour on the West Bank of the River Jordan.

From the time of the incident described in the next chapter our stay in Jerusalem was peaceful and on the whole uneventful.

CHAPTER V: THE JERUSALEM INCIDENT

Early in June Brigadier Green went to England on leave and I took over the Brigade, retaining at the same time command of the Regiment. I was responsible, roughly speaking, for a stretch of frontier running from Ramallah in the North to Hebron in the South, and for the defence of Jerusalem.

Nine kilometres inside the Jordan frontier, in the district of Tulkarm, lies the village of Azzoun. On the night of 28th June a small patrol of Israeli shock troops infiltrated to the village and attacked soldiers sleeping in their tent, spraying them with sub-machine-guns, killing and wounding. Part of 3 Regiment, a bedouin battalion, was stationed there at that time, and fortunately the commander, Major Atta Ali, had collected most of his men for some purpose behind the village; with them he quickly came to the rescue. One of the raiders was wounded and captured. I saw him afterwards in hospital; he was typical of the young thugs who in former days formed the hard core of the Stern Gang.

This shameful outrage was rightly condemned by the Mixed Armistice Commission, but, as will appear hereafter, it never made the headlines in the world press.

June 30th was a very hot day indeed. I spent it in a landing-craft on the Dead Sea, which is 1275 feet below sea level. In the evening I returned, hot and tired, and was lying in the bath when the telephone rang. Wondering whatever could have induced me to become a soldier, I climbed out and, wrapped in a towel, went to the telephone, fully expecting to hear that

Brigade H.Q. wanted to know where the monthly training report had got to.

I picked up the receiver. It was a cadet, Muhamad Rkheimeh, who was temporarily in command at the Citadel, as the senior officer there had gone on a course. The Israeli post in a building known as the Green House, or the Clarke House, near the North-West corner of the Old City, had opened a heavy fire in the direction of the Frères' School. I questioned him narrowly as to the amount of firing, told him he was not to shoot back and that I would join him as soon as I could.

Before I could put down the receiver the signaller on the central exchange told me that my post at Deir Abu Tor wanted to talk to me; this is about a mile from the Frères' School. Sergeant Ahmed Ishtewi was in command there, a good instructor, but no thunderbolt in action; he also was under a heavy fire. I warned him that I would have his blood if he returned the fire without my orders. A few seconds later Cadet Shayem Oudeh, commanding in the Musrara, rang up. It was the same story. I repeated the same orders.

Nothing like this had ever happened since the Regiment came to Jerusalem the previous February. Although we lived in many places within point-blank range of the Israelis we had only had one very minor incident, as related in the previous chapter. We had always had the strictest orders not to fire. The telephone rang again. It was Muhamad Rkheimeh to say that the Citadel itself was now receiving a hot fire.

I rang up the Regiment and got on to my second-in-command, Saoud Rashdan. I told him to get down to the Citadel as quickly as he could, find out what the hell was going on, and ensure that there was no firing without my orders. I would join him as soon as possible. Next I got on to the Chief Clerk, Fuad Shahin, and told him that he was to stay at

Regimental Headquarters beside the telephone until I personally told him to fall out. I told him to get hold of Ahmed Qasim, my interpreter, and send him to my house right away; and at the same time sent the sentry running off into the dark to fetch Juma'a, who lived further up the hill.

Then I remembered that Colonel Hutton, the Chief of Staff, was spending the night in Nablus, and I rang through to him and told him what was happening. I explained that the firing had broken out simultaneously all along the front, which could only have happened if the Israelis were working to a prearranged Zero Hour. I asked him under what circumstances we could fire back.

He received my news with his accustomed calm and replied that "the orders are to fire back bren for bren, round for round, and mortar bomb for mortar bomb", but on no account were we to fire more than the enemy did. This order I passed on to the Regiment. I also rang up Turki Hussein, the Brigade-Major, told him the form as far as I knew it, and asked him to pass on the information to Division and H.Q. Arab Legion.

By the time I was dressed, Ahmed and Juma'a had arrived. "To St. Stephen's Gate," I said. We drove down the hill, into the Wadi Joz, the black mass of the Hebrew University in the Jewish enclave looming up on our right. No firing was coming from that direction. We dashed up the hill, Juma'a trying to push the accelerator through the floor, swung round a couple of corners, under the arch of St. Stephen's Gate and into the Via Dolorosa. I stopped the car at the road junction beyond the Ottoman bank and, followed by Ahmed, walked through the streets towards the Damascus Gate. Many shops were still open in the dimly lit streets. The bullets were cracking overhead, and the people were gathering in excited groups. We spoke to them as we went along, saying "Good evening" and "It is nothing" and so on, while they pointed at us and said, "The Qaid, the Qaid of Kateba Tis'a."

We reached the Damascus Gate and made our way up the steps on to the wall. A bedouin challenged us. "I am the Qaid," I said. "Ask him what the bloody password is." Armed with this useful piece of information we pushed on along the sentry-walk. The soldiers manning the gate were standing to at the loopholes on the wall. They were not firing. There were still a lot of bullets flying about, but, covered by the wall, the men were fairly safe. "Don't fire. It is nothing." It was actually rather noisy. I was glad to find that Ahmed Qasim did not care.

As we neared the Latin Convent, we came across Muhamad Qdeini, son of an Iraqi sheikh, a lance-corporal. He Commanded a bren team. "Are you all right?" They were. We all peered over the wall. The night was very black. From the Israeli lines came an unceasing flicker of rifle shots, and occasional bursts from a light automatic. Then there were two loud thuds. Mortars. "Well, don't fire." "There is nothing to fire at," he replied. "Don't fire, don't fire."

As we neared the New Gate the firing grew noisier. The Israelis in the hospice of Notre Dame de France were shooting at good deal. I climbed down a wooden ladder and went into one of my platoon headquarters to ring up Glubb Pasha and tell him what was going on. There was such a racket coming from the Notre Dame that I could hardly hear myself speak.

Ahmed and I went on through the now deserted streets of the Christian quarter and joined Saoud at the Citadel. There was still some firing going on, on both sides. Saoud and I agreed that it was a waste of ammunition, and gave Rkheimeh orders to cease fire. I told him that the men between the

Damascus and New Gates were not firing when I reached them, and that I had told them not to.

General Cooke was on leave and Brigadier Galletly was in command of the Division. I rang him up from the Citadel, thinking that 2 Brigade Headquarters might not have succeeded in getting through to him. He asked me if I wanted any reinforcements. I said that I did not. I had alerted my reserve companies but I had not brought them up because the presence of more troops would only add to the casualties. For the same reason I had not called out the National Guard, though a number of them had reported for duty. I told him that it was quite clear that this was merely a fire-fight, laid on, presumably, with the object of provoking an incident. I added that in my opinion the Israelis were not trying to capture the Old City or to make a serious attack.

Next I rang up Commander Hutchinson, the head of the Mixed Armistice Commission, who said that he had been in touch with the other side to try to arrange a cease-fire. I told him what I had myself seen and done, and that I would give the necessary orders to my own troops.

It was about 9.30 p.m. when I left Saoud in charge in my command post and climbed up to the Minaret Tower. There was a lull. No flashes broke the blackness opposite. We could just see the tower of the Y.M.C.A. against the night sky, above the solid mass of the King David Hotel. Hardly a light was to be seen anywhere in the western suburbs. Twenty minutes went by. The night was delightfully cool after the heat of the Dead Sea. It looked as if the cease-fire was effective this time. It was nearly ten o'clock when the shooting began again. The bedouin did not reply from the walls of the Citadel.

I returned to the command post and found Rkheimeh in an ill-temper, sullen and resentful. He was commanding a company for the first time and was flapping slightly. Saoud was laughing at him. We had tea.

On this night the defence of the Mandelbaum Gate was entrusted to a cadet of the Sirhan tribe, Addad Msayeh. A cheerful boy, then perhaps nineteen years old, he is not very big even for a bedouin. He was not considered a military genius; few of the Sirhan are — a pity, for they are a robust people. He had a platoon, mostly recruits, and a lance-corporal was acting as his platoon sergeant. The company commander had taken the precaution of surrounding himself with senior N.C.O.s in his headquarters! There is nothing like a crisis for finding people out. The lance-corporal was a clever haderi from Shobek, Mamoud Suleiman; he was usually caught for a job in the Canteen, because he could read and write, and he had the added virtue that he did not mind being shot at. Among the privates was one Abbas Moussa, who had been reduced from full corporal for some trifling offence, and had asked to be transferred to 9 Regiment; he acted as a section commander. The recruits included Abdulla Salameh, one of the Belgawi from near Amman, who was distinguished for his coolness on this occasion.

The position at the Mandelbaum Gate was a very dangerous one when we first went to Jerusalem. It was sited for defence from the front, but there was no all-round defence. We had changed all that in the previous four months, and had held manning exercises daily so that everyone knew his task. There was a very strong post supporting the left flank of the Mandelbaum, but at the time of which I am writing there was nothing to its right. Needless to say this post came in for its full share of attention. The Israelis fired on it from three sides. This only came to light next day, because fortunately it did not worry Addad. Saoud and I rang him up several times to see how he was getting on, and received cheerful reassurances. Shayem Oudeh, his company commander, being a sensitive sort of person, did not care to visit him at night, and so it was not until next day that we knew what a noisy evening he had spent. Luckily we had bricked up all the windows in the direction of Israel, and so if some of the bedu lost their beauty sleep, at least nobody got hurt.

At five to twelve the Israelis sent fourteen 2-inch mortar bombs into the Armenian quarter. They whistled over the Citadel where I was sitting talking to Saoud Rashdan, and wondering why they did not go to bed. The bombs made a great crump in the narrow streets of the Old City, and I thought, until I saw the bits next morning, that they must be 3-inch. The police sentry standing guard at the main gate of the Police H.Q., the Kishlak, was struck in the leg by a splinter. Some of the bombs fell in St. James', the Armenian Cathedral; others damaged Christ Church. These were not the first mortar bombs to land in the Old City that night, but it was the biggest concentration. By about half-past twelve the fourth attempt of the M.A.C. to arrange a cease fire appeared to have succeeded. All became quiet. Leaving Rkheimeh to sulk in peace, Ahmed and I walked back through the empty streets to the hospital, where our Land-Rover was parked. We had a look at the wounded policeman who was fairly comfortable; then Juma'a drove us back up the Mount of Olives. When I got home my wife told me that at one time the firing had seemed so close that she thought the Israelis had come out of the Hadassah and attacked Et Tur.

According to Israeli sources, eight of their casualties on this night were hit during the first hour. As ill luck would have it one of them, Rabbi Moshe Goldberg, a delegate from France to a Jewish World Congress, died of his wounds. He was hit in the head and face by a bomb which exploded in the Eretz Yisrael Hotel in the Mea Shearsim quarter.

1ST JULY

When I awoke on the morning of 1st July, I heard that all had been quiet during the early hours. I had two things to do: to write a report on the events of the previous night; and to visit Brigade and see how Turki Hussein was getting on. I called at Regimental Headquarters on the way, and found that all was in order. Saoud Rashdan was his imperturbable self. We decided to leave Fuad in charge at R.H.Q., and set up a Command Post in the Musrara.

The Old City with its massive walls seemed safe enough. If the Israelis were going to try anything it might be further North, where in those days our defences left something to be desired. I set off for Brigade Headquarters in the Humber. I found that Turki had risen to the occasion and had everything under control. Nothing was happening on the rest of our front, so I decided to stay in Jerusalem myself, and to leave Turki in charge at Brigade. His main task was to pass on information to H.Q. Arab Legion, Division, and our other two battalions. I told him to see to it that forward posts and patrols in the Jerusalem area were found by regular soldiers and not National Guards, whose fire control might conceivably leave something to be desired. The National Guard were a reserve force raised for local defence and to guard frontier villages. They had not the training or the equipment of regulars, and it had been reported to me that some of them had been shooting at street lights in the Wadi Joz on the previous evening.

A message came asking me to call at the headquarters of the Jordan M.A.C., as the Minister of Defence wanted a report from me.

As we drove back into the Sheikh Jarrah quarter all was still quiet. We slowed down for the sharp corner by the Police Post — a most unpleasant place when any firing is going on — and crossed the Wadi Joz, now sheltered from Israeli bullets by a high wall, passed the American Colony, which had collected a few bullets the night before, and the New Cinema with its enormous glass front facing trustingly towards Israel. All was quiet.

During the morning people were passing through the Mandelbaum Gate in the normal way. A party of thirty tourists crossed from the Old City into Israel.

On arriving at the headquarters of the Jordan M.A.C. delegation I was introduced to Anwar Nuseibeh, who is considered by many to be the ablest man in Jordanian political life. He is still young, perhaps forty-five. A graduate of Cambridge University where he read law, and a tennis blue, he took a prominent part in the 1948 fighting. He distinguished himself by his courageous leadership but had the misfortune to lose a leg. A citizen of Jerusalem, where his house is actually in the front line, he had been in Amman when the Israelis opened fire. After a hasty conference with Tewfik Abul Huda, the Prime Minister, he hurried back to Jerusalem.

Though he was well-known to me by repute, I had never before met the Defence Minister, but I found in him a courteous listener, and a man who thoroughly appreciated my problems. I found him sitting with Dr. Heikal. Major Muhamad Ishaq, a Circassian, who was the senior officer there, ushered me in, and I was asked to sit down. Coffee was brought. I explained what had been happening. They were delighted with the way the troops had behaved, and the firm line which we had taken.

But meanwhile, the Israelis, for obvious reasons, were first with the news. *The Times* was only one of the newspapers which carried their version of the incident. Moshe Sharett, the Israel Prime Minister, lost no time in issuing a statement which began:

> "The peace of Jerusalem was wantonly violated last night when the Arab Legion opened fire on Israel's capital along the entire sector of the armistice lines within the city.
>
> It was a deliberate attack, without the slightest provocation, obviously planned and centrally directed."

He was quick off his marks — perhaps almost too quick.

Meanwhile the heads of the Christian communities in the Old City were cabling to the Pope complaining that an Israel shell had landed near the Church of the Holy Sepulchre. And in Amman, Issa Bandak, the Under Secretary for Foreign Affairs, called on John Richmond, the Advisor to the British Embassy, and asked if Britain, the U.S.A, and France would raise the question of this attack with the Security Council.

When I had finished explaining the situation to the Defence Minister, he told me that he considered that any further aggression on the part of the Israelis should be met with equal force. "An eye for an eye, and a tooth for a tooth" is a popular proverb among the Arabs, and not a bad one at that. A number of journalists had arrived and I was asked to explain to them what was going on, for it was feared that as usual the Israelis would win the war of words. I had just said that in my opinion there would be no more trouble, when there was a long burst of machine-gun fire from the direction of the Notre Dame, followed by a good deal of small-arms fire. It was 11 o'clock (Jordan time). The fire was aimed at the crowded square outside the Damascus Gate — the point where some twenty people had been struck down in April 1953. Since that time we had built a thick and high wall to cover this area, which happily was nearly complete. On this occasion only one person was hit: it was nonetheless a murderous attempt, and my cook, Ali Muhamad Ali, who was shopping, nearly collapsed. He arrived home grey in the face, with his ferocious moustache at half-mast, and reported it as the massacre of no less than twenty innocent victims. He had seen it all with his own eyes from his vantage point under a bus.

In one of the towers of the Damascus Gate I had a Vickers gun. A Hejazi corporal, Saleh Ibrahim Shweish, was in charge and as soon as he saw what was happening he sent a belt of bullets streaming into the breach in the East wall of the Notre Dame. At once their fire slackened. This was enough. I gave orders to cease fire, in the hope that the Israelis would do the same. At the same time Commander Hutchinson got to work once more and arranged "an unconditional and sincere cease fire", which was to come into effect as from 5.30 p.m. Gradually the firing died away again and I did not hear any shooting during the early afternoon.

Hutchinson placed two observers on the Y.M.C.A. building, and I agreed that he could put an officer on the roof of the Frères' School, an excellent O.P., but a building which we never occupied ourselves because we did not wish to give the Israelis any excuse for shooting it up. The other side refused to allow the U.N. observers to use that matchless vantage point, the Notre Dame. The implications are obvious.

In the afternoon General Bennike presided over a meeting of the M.A.C. Sgan Aluv A. Shalev and Mr. Y. Tekoa represented Israel, while Dr. Heikal and Major Muhamad Ishaq spoke for Jordan. Commander Hutchinson, the usual chairman, was present but took no part. The Israelis had been boycotting the

M.A.C. ever since the Scorpion's Pass incident in 1953. They were indignant that Jordan had not been condemned for a massacre which may well have been an episode in a war between the Stern Gang and some of its rivals. General Bennike pointed out that there was precedent for such a meeting, as one had been held in the days of his predecessor, General W. E. Riley, U.S. Army, when, in April 1953, Israeli soldiers had shot down people at the Damascus Gate. The General suggested firstly that both sides forbid and punish future sniping. Secondly that each should order an unconditional cease fire, and thirdly that they should report future breaches to the U.N. organization for immediate investigation.

In addition he appealed to the two Governments to make it clear that they had no intention of starting military operations, and to withdraw any reinforcements who might have come in on Wednesday or Thursday, so as to relax the tension. *The Jerusalem Post* later commented that Dr. Heikal had not given the numbers of the Arab casualties, or reinforcements. There was no point in talking about our reinforcements. There were none. The Israelis admitted that they had brought up more troops, but claimed that reinforcements deployed in the City were within the limits of the Armistice agreement; they were entitled to have two battalions in the area. There were probably not more than two brigades, 6 and 16.

According to *The Jerusalem Post* this meeting was still in session when firing was heard from the direction of Deir Abu Tor, and an officer was sent out to investigate. This was about 5.30 Israeli time, or 4.30 Jordan time. At 5.30 there was no firing going on, and I drove in the Humber through the Dung Gate and round to the Citadel. The Israeli sentries on the Church of the Dormition did not fire at us and so I presumed that this truce was going to work. I saw Rkheimeh and warned him not to allow any shooting unless the enemy were actually scaling the walls, and drove away again.

Deir Abu Tor was much in my mind. It was at that time rather a weak position, overlooked by the Israeli posts on the top of the hill. I was afraid they had had a bad night up there, and thought it a good opportunity to go and see them. "Well, Ahmed," I said, "this is where we take our lives in our hands and go and call on Ahmed Ishtewi." I do not suppose he was any more pleased than I was. We drove out of the Dung Gate, down through Silwan, the old Siloam, and up the hill towards Deir Abu Tor. After a time the road comes into full view of the Church of the Dormition, where, as I take it, the Israelis keep a company. The Humber seemed the size of a haycart and about as fast. Nobody fired, and with a mixture of disappointment and relief we reached the cover of the houses.

Leaving Juma'a with the car Ahmed and I walked up to the left-hand forward position. Here Muhamad Sadoun, an Iraqi lance-corporal, with big white teeth and a hawk nose, was in command. He was a very good, level-headed chap, and was in great heart, not impressed by his neighbours further up the hill, who as ill-luck would have it had wounded one of his men. A bullet had come in one of the loopholes, and hit this soldier, who was standing in the middle of the room. A chance in a thousand. Blood was soaking into the mud floor. Ahmed and I talked to the soldiers for a bit, told them the situation in the City, and explained that the trouble was now over.

After a while with Muhamad Sadoun we walked on up the hill towards the headquarters. There came shots from high up on our left, and almost at once a woman hastened towards us, pointing and talking shrilly as Arab women do when they are excited. "What the hell is she on about?" "She says a woman has just been shot beside your Humber, sir." I looked at my watch, it was twenty minutes past six. The "unconditional and sincere cease fire" had lasted fifty minutes.

The first victim of this new outbreak, a young Palestinian girl, had been standing only a yard from the car. Some gallant Israeli rifleman in one of the houses drew a bead on her at a range of perhaps two hundred yards and shot her down. No costume could be more distinctive than her picturesque Arab dress. It would not be possible, in daylight and at such close range, to have supposed her to be a soldier. She collapsed moaning in the dust before the eyes of half a dozen villagers, who were too thunderstruck to raise a finger. The sniper kept up his fusillade and nobody dared stir. It was left to Juma'a to rescue her. Sauntering across the road in his arrogant way, he picked her up in his arms and carried her to the cover of a house.

Followed by Ahmed I went on up to the headquarters. We knew where most of the Israeli posts were and I took care to keep a house between them and us. The post was only a matter of fifty yards from the enemy on top of the hill, but nobody saw us arrive. Peering from the loopholes, we could not pick out this new enemy — he was probably well inside one of the rooms opposite.

Ghazi Tallaq, the Signals Corporal, got me through to Division. I stood, telephone in hand, looking out of the window towards the houses which hid the Humber and telling Ski Galletly what had happened. About a hundred yards below and over to the right I could see an old man walking slowly up the road. As I watched there came another volley of shots, the dust flicked up round his feet, he staggered and ran for the cover of a house. I doubt if the news of any incident ever reached headquarters more quickly. Once more the divisional commander offered us reinforcements, but they were not needed. It was at half-past six when these last shootings took place. The old man, the father of the wounded girl, had been hit in the foot.

Ahmed Ishtewi had the support of two good N.C.O.s, Ghazi Tallaq, a stout-hearted man, though a great talker, and Salameh Haza'a. The latter, then a lance-corporal, was an Iraqi, and the best type of young bedu N.C.O., alert, cheerful and fit. I looked round the defences, and then had another look at the Israeli positions. The light was in our eyes, and we could see no movement. We had tea. I talked to Brigade and R.H.Q. on the telephone, telling them what had occurred. All was quiet both here and on the rest of the front.

At about five minutes to seven we heard heavy firing, which seemed to come from the direction of the Musrara.

It must have been at this time that cars carrying U.N. observers came under fire from the Israelis in the Street of the Prophets, which runs through the Musrara quarter. The cars were white with "U.N." painted in huge black letters on the sides. Despite the fate of Count Bernadotte in 1948[6] I refuse to believe that the Israeli high command would be so inept as to order such an outrage. The fact is that their troops had got out of hand. Commander Hutchinson was quickly on the scene, and after a wireless conversation with his officers on the other side, managed to get the firing stopped after about twenty minutes, and his officers extricated.

Soon afterwards mortar bombs began to fall on the summit of the Mount of Olives. We could see some of them plainly, and as I lived behind the Mount of Olives, I rang up my wife to find out how things were going at home.

---

[6] Count Bernadotte was shot by some Jews in Jerusalem while endeavouring to negotiate an armistice.

"They are mortaring the top of the Mount of Olives," I said.

"Like hell they are, they are coming right over!"

About five went over, one hitting the wall of the Russian convent. The nearest fell perhaps a hundred and fifty yards from our house and I got a running commentary on this, interrupted at one stage by Ali Muhamad Ali, who ran into the room where my wife was telephoning shouting, "To the Jebel, to the Jebel". The women of the Khurshaid family came rushing out from the flat below ours, clutching their numerous progeny to their bosoms and departed up the hill with piercing cries of "Aiee! Aieee!" My batman, Ali, was stumping about in full equipment, rifle in hand, the light of battle in his eye; while Osman stood at the back door, shifting slowly and uneasily from one foot to the other, moaning like an injured camel.

As soon as it got dark we left Deir Abu Tor, taking the wounded man and Ghazi Tallaq's wife. On our way we met Abdulla Dahil leading a platoon up to reinforce the garrison.

After a time the Israelis, who, as I heard later from a reasonably reliable source, were firing from the Mamilla cemetery, dropped their range and began to put bombs into the Old City. The United Nations observers afterwards found that these bombs were from a 3-inch mortar. From the rate of fire I think that only one gun was firing; I counted thirty-one bombs, but some say thirty-seven were received.

The 3-inch mortar platoon in 9 Regiment was quite efficient, and I may say that I was much tempted to order five rounds gunfire. However, I considered that if I did so the Israeli casualties would be mostly civilians.

It seems that there was a midnight conference at Government House on the 1st. Next day *The Jerusalem Post* reported:

"that Rav-Aluf Dayan explained to General Bennike that Wednesday's attack had been well prepared and many units of the Arab Legion had taken part."

General Moshe Dayan, who lost an eye serving in the British forces in the last war, was and is the Chief of Staff of the Israeli army. His intelligence about the Arab Legion evidently left something to be desired.

The Israelis said at the time that they had suffered twenty-two casualties by the evening of this day. They alleged that five were reported after half-past six when the unconditional cease fire had begun, and that four of these were at Deir Abu Tor. I visited my posts there at that time. No Israelis were showing themselves. My soldiers were not firing.

The Arab casualties by this time were approximately one killed and eleven wounded, including two soldiers and one policeman.

2ND JULY

On this day there was sporadic firing, but during the night there had been an exchange of shots between the Church of the Dormition, and our post on the Gate of the Prophet David, and an Israeli soldier had been killed.

At about 8 a.m. a bedouin sentry in the Citadel shot a man near the foot of the City Wall in No Man's Land. This poor wretch had started out from Israeli-held territory at about 6 a.m. and the soldier had watched him as he crawled forward about a hundred yards in two hours, carrying a suspicious bundle. The sentry thought he was going to place a charge against the wall. The man, who was poorly dressed, was, I believe, never identified. The Israelis claimed later that he was either blind or mentally unbalanced, which was presumably true. How the Israeli border guards allowed him to wander through their front-line does not appear. I contacted the M.A.C. so that a party could go and pick him up, guaranteeing a safe conduct for them so long as a U.N. observer conducted them. The body was taken away without further unpleasantness.

At about eleven o'clock an old Arab porter was shot dead in the Old City in a street running south from the New Gate. Riflemen posted in the Notre Dame, not a hundred yards away were responsible. They can have had no doubt that he was a civilian. I was in the Citadel when I was told of this, and went there immediately. There were a number of civilians, a handful of police and the Swedish Major Peter Schwartz of the U.N. observers. Bob Smithson and I walked down the right of the street where there was a little cover, and looked at the body. The man was dead. The Israelis kept on shooting. I counted ten more shots from the Notre Dame during the next hour. Eventually Schwartz brought in the body under a flag of truce.

My men did not return the fire from the Notre Dame on this occasion. I had given orders that no bren was to have a magazine on the gun, and no rifleman was to have a round up the spout. I went along the wall from man to man, and saw that my orders were obeyed. In this way I was able to make certain that if there was firing it came from the other side.

It was not only from the Notre Dame that the firing came. Traffic through the Mandelbaum Gate was held up for a time and the Latin Patriarch, who was on his way to a service at Ain Karim was delayed.

On 2nd July, the State Department, with admirable impartiality released identical broadsides in the direction of Jordan and Israel.

"The U.S. Government has been informed that widespread heavy firing broke out in Jerusalem on June 30th, and has since continued intermittently, reportedly even after an agreement on a ceasefire was reached at a meeting of the Israel-Jordan Mixed Armistice Commission on July 1st.

The U.S. Government deplores this serious outbreak of violence in the Holy City, with its attendant loss of life, and urges the governments of Jordan and Israel to take immediate steps to ensure the observance of the cease-fire."

In Amman the Prime Minister, Tewfik Abul Huda, received Monseigneur Tlesta, the Papal Nuncio in Jordan who was reported to have expressed the Pope's anxiety over the Israeli aggression to which the Holy City was subject.

3RD JULY

General Bennike now issued a statement in which he thanked both sides for their co-operation in putting an end to the senseless shooting, expressing his sympathy with the victims, and hoping that the cease-fire would not be broken again. This message was all loving kindness. It praised the U.N. Military Observers, very reasonably; it also praised the authorities of Jordan and Israel. In fact it got nobody anywhere. And nobody was pleased since both parties were hoping to see the other condemned in no uncertain terms.

There was no further shooting on this day, although activity on the political front was considerable. King Hussein postponed his trip to Europe, and presided over a meeting of the Cabinet, which discussed the situation. In Beirut the Egyptian Minister of Guidance, Salah Salem — the dancing Major — announced that the Egyptian army was ready to take the field in our support, which was a great relief to us! Anwar Nuseibeh was quoted in "Falastin", praising the Arab Legion "for teaching the Jews a good lesson." Five Arabs had been killed and twenty-six wounded, including two soldiers and a policeman.

As far as I was concerned the main event of the day was the meeting in Jerusalem of the Jordan Supreme Defence Council. Glubb Pasha; Jamal Toukan, the Foreign Minister; Anwar Nuseibeh and many senior officers were there to study the measures necessary to prevent future aggression. Glubb Pasha asked me how much ammunition, and particularly how many 2-inch mortar bombs had been fired. A check of the ammunition of the various platoons showed that three had fired their 2-inch mortars. This was on the night of the 30th June, and in answer to mortar fire from the Israelis. Altogether fourteen bombs had been expended mostly in the Musrara and at Deir Abu Tor.

In order to avoid constant friction it was decided that an effort should be made to demilitarize two religious foundations, which were held by the Israelis. These were the Church of the Dormition and the Notre Dame de France (see plan). Unfortunately nothing came of the project. While they are occupied by Israeli soldiers a fire-fight may develop at any time. If the Arabs do not return the fire, they must be swept off the Old City wall, and can no longer observe the No Man's Land and the dead ground at the foot of the wall.

After the meeting messages were sent to the various Western diplomatic envoys, protesting against this unprovoked attack.

When the meeting broke up, that irrepressible person Madhat Nashashibi, correspondent of the Beirut *Daily Star* came bouncing up to the Pasha, determined to get a few words out of him. He quoted him as saying that the "Arabs cannot be sure of Israel's intentions," which was true enough and added that Glubb had "ordered his troops to immediately return any Israeli fire." I must say that that was not how I understood the orders I had received. However, Madhat is a keen journalist. The poor blind or mentally deficient man shot the morning before was promoted to be an Israeli officer.

Earlier in the proceedings Moshe Dayan had threatened to renew hostilities along the whole of the six hundred and fifty kilometre front. On this day, rather curiously, the Israelis denied that this threat had been made.

It was quite clear to me that the outbreak on the night of the 30th was merely a fire-fight. Patrols may have advanced towards our posts in some places, but on the whole the Israelis had confined their activities to shooting. Nevertheless, they had admitted reinforcing their garrison. At the end of this meeting I received a hint from a peculiarly well-placed observer that these reinforcements had been very considerable. This person, who was greatly concerned that there should be no further outbreak had a notion that the real coup was yet to come. Naturally I passed on this information for what it was worth.

Meanwhile despite my repeated assurances that reinforcements were not required, 2 Regiment had been moved to the West Bank, and was concentrated near Talat-ed-Damm, over ten miles from Jerusalem where they were in a position to support us in the event of an Israeli advance. The C.O., Lt.-Col. Khaled-es-Sahen, came forward to see me, and receive his orders.

The afternoon was warm and no shots broke the truce on either side. But the tension remained. Both sides stood to with their eyes glued to the loopholes, glaring at each other. I well remember watching for some minutes an Israeli soldier creeping about on the roof of a house near the Mandelbaum Gate. Bending double he advanced rifle in hand to the cover of a wall of sandbags, which covered him from a post we occupied some forty yards to his front. I was perhaps three hundred yards away from him, and beside me were two snipers, Irshaid Irheiba and Tobash Nahar, with rifles with telescopic sights. He was taking such elaborate precautions to protect himself from his front, that it was a grave temptation to put one past his ear and see what he did about it.

But the tension remained. Were the Israelis just taking their soldiering a bit seriously, or was something up? A nod is as good as a wink, and the information received was from a source second to none.

A little later I happened to be having tea with the British Consul-General and I mentioned my doubts to him. A curious episode followed, "I've got a direct line to the Civil Governor on the other side," he said — Dr. Berian, I believe his name was — "Shall I ring him up and ask him?" It seemed to me an excellent idea. The most categorical assurances were forthcoming that nothing was farther from our neighbours' minds than any kind of trespass! The assurance was clearly worth something. After all H.M.G. might not be terribly pleased if its representatives were told barefaced lies. It may appear rather ridiculous to ring up the enemy and ask if they are going to attack you. However, this was more like manoeuvres than a battle. There were so many umpires!

It may be that the incident did good. At least I could take a risk that one would not normally take in war, and let my sentries pass the night without magazines on their automatics, or rounds in their rifles.

4TH JULY

There had been no further outbreak during the night and even on the Israeli side of the line things were getting back to normal. From the Old City walls one could see the buses running on their normal routes. I was told that the people were returning to their houses in the Musrara quarter and in Old Jaffa Street. Schools re-opened. Residents of the western suburbs who, on Wednesday night or on Thursday, had paid as much as £13 for a seat in a taxi to Tel Aviv, could now return home for the normal fare.

The U.N. observers completed their investigations in Israel. They were allegedly shown mortar bombs with British markings. It is understood also that the windows of the King David Hotel had suffered.

By the 6th things were back to normal. Israeli soldiers posted in the Notre Dame building hurled stones at our men on the Old City wall, and Muhamad Ishaq lodged a complaint with the M.A.C.

In the Knesset Mr. Lavon, the Defence Minister, admitted that the Israelis had used a medium mortar during the incident, but little else. "Lavon Flays Arab Version of Jerusalem Shooting" was the headline in *The Jerusalem Post* next day.

On 12th July, asked for a statement in the House of Commons, Mr. Selwyn Lloyd said:

> "From the conflicting reports which we received it was not clear who fired the first shot in the fighting which broke out in Jerusalem on June 30th. In view of the danger of this outbreak leading to even more serious trouble between Israel and Jordan and because of the likelihood of damage to the Holy Places in Jerusalem, Her Majesty's Government and the United States and French Governments urged both sides to exercise restraint and assist the efforts of the U.N. Truce Supervision Organisation to arrange a cease-fire. The shooting eventually ceased at about noon on July 2nd. The Mixed Armistice Commission met in Jerusalem on July 11th, and after statements by General Bennike, Chief of Staff of the United Nations Truce Supervision Organisation, and the

Israeli delegate, adjourned till today. General Bennike said that the incident had cost the lives of nine people and that fifty-two others had been wounded. He stated that the Truce Supervision Organisation had obtained no evidence that either side had planned an offensive and that it was not clear who fired the first shot. Lack of control over border guards by both sides may have been the basic cause of the outbreak. He appealed to the Jordanian and Israeli delegations not to cloud the air with mutual recriminations but rather to try to agree over measures designed to make a recurrence of such incidents impossible. To this end General Bennike made some specific suggestions which, I hope, will receive the serious attention of the delegation of the two sides. General Bennike concluded his statement by saying that Israel and Jordan are in the eyes of all the world the trustees of Jerusalem, and it is only through their own most earnest efforts that this important centre of population with its Holy Places and its religious and cultural institutions can be preserved in the interest of the two states themselves and of all the nations of the world. Her Majesty's Government wish to associate themselves most sincerely with these words."

During the days of the Jerusalem Incident the Israelis were almost the least of my problems. They did not advance, and probably never intended to. They fired off a great quantity of ammunition, but mostly into the air. They hit one of my soldiers, who later recovered; wounded a policeman, not seriously; and killed one soldier who was on leave. I do not underrate the Israeli Army, by current Middle East standards they are above average. But I was glad I was not dealing with the Germans or the Japanese, in which case, no doubt, our casualties would have been a good deal heavier.

Nor was the Regiment my chief problem. Saoud Rashdan was quite capable of running that. We held our line with the troops who were there when the shooting started, and except for patrols, changed nothing. There were no troop movements, so it was not very complicated. The men were in good heart, and as most of them had never been in action before it did them good to be shot at. They did not seem to mind.

The Jerusalem National Guard were and are, in my opinion, much above the average. Their commander, Asser Bey Majali always co-operated one hundred per cent with 9 Regiment. On the night of 30th June more than a hundred of his men reported for duty at his R.H.Q., and they were dead keen to man the walls and let off their pieces at the neighbours. However, I had not the least intention of indulging their humour, and Asser Bey, with his usual tact, patted them on the back and sent them off home. Those National Guards who normally went out on patrol, were disarmed and replaced by regulars. I preferred to deal with my own Regiment only. If they fired without my orders I could punish them.

The Jerusalem Police were commanded by Qaid Abdel Haleem Bey Saket. Our relations were always excellent, and I do not remember that during those days any problem arose; the police carried on with their normal job. As far as Brigade Headquarters was concerned I left everything to Turki Hussein for three days; if he wanted anything he knew where to find me.

In addition to all these I had to deal directly with H.Q. Arab Legion, with the Pasha or Jim Hutton; and also with Division, with Galletly or Luard. All naturally wanted to be kept in the picture, which took time. The Defence Minister, living on the spot, also wished to know what was going on. Again it was absolutely essential to keep Dr. Heikal and Muhamad Ishaq informed. They had to deal with the Mixed Armistice Commission, which, of course, was not possible if they did not have all the facts at their finger tips.

Commander Hutchinson and the U.N. Military Observers naturally demanded a good deal of attention. This was only reasonable since they were running considerable personal risks in trying to keep the peace. Colonel Norgaard, David Ely, John Debar and Peter Schwartz all had their quota of close shaves during these three days.

Lastly the Press insisted on a little attention. Wynne of Associated Press and Kenneth Love, the Middle East correspondent of *The New York Times*, were in the City. The latter paper, I understand, is owned by Jews, not all Zionists, though the editor was thought to be one. It seemed to me that there was no harm in letting these people know what was going on. The Arabs usually get a bad press in the Western world. The Legion had nothing to lose. It was from this time that *The Times* first had a correspondent in Jerusalem (Jordan side) as well as Jerusalem (Israel side) and he also interviewed me.

The people of Jerusalem were very good indeed; there was no panic, no exodus; few shops were shut. There was a mood of sober satisfaction, because, for once the Legion had struck back. "El ain bil ain, wa es sinn bi sinn."[7] In the words of Hassan el Kateb, the Governor of the Old City: "the people of Jerusalem have decided to remain in the City and defend it to the last."

Then there were the more numerous representatives of Arab newspapers. I never knew when I would not be ambushed by Madhat Nashashibi, and his tame photographer. "Can I tell the *Daily Star* that the Arab Legion is pouring in reinforcements?"

---

[7] An eye for an eye and a tooth for a tooth.

"NO." "Can I quote you as saying that you welcome a Jewish aggression?" "NO." "Then can I say that a highly placed military source says...." "My dear Madhat, I know perfectly well that you will say whatever comes into your head." "Colonel you are choking."

The United Nations Organisation did not condemn Israel for this piece of aggression. It produced a long report, containing no account by either commander. If you were going to write up the battle of Waterloo I presume your first step would be to see what Wellington and Napoleon had to say on the subject! Most of the statements were from casualties on either side; the one person who never knows what has happened in a battle is someone who was hit!

Only once previously had men of 9 Regiment opened fire since they came to Jerusalem in February. That was in the Musrara incident already described. They would not wantonly open fire on anyone. The bedouin does not delight in bloodshed, for traditionally he is afraid of becoming involved in expensive blood feuds. If the Israelis have wronged the Palestinian Arabs, they have had little contact with the bedouin, who know little about them. Once I asked a soldier whether he disliked the Israelis, and was somewhat disconcerted when he replied: "All men are brothers."

It remains to decide whether the incident was a spontaneous affair caused by some "trigger-happy" Israeli border guard, or whether it was laid on by their General Staff. It is a question that I have long pondered, and I think that the latter solution is the more probable. How else did Moshe Sharett manage to come out so pat with his statement on July 1st? How else did their version so quickly reach the front pages in the U.S.A, and in Great Britain? How else could the Israelis have escaped the indignation which would have been aroused against them had the Azzoun incident become known to the world? If the plan was not carefully preconcerted how is it that the firing broke out all along the line at the same instant?

That the incident was the result of careful planning I have no doubt. But I am positive it was not planned in Jordan.

The United Nations officers spared no effort and took every risk to bring about an armistice, but the ultimate executive power did not lie with them. They could not give direct orders to platoon and section commanders. I could. Indeed by chance (on the Jordanian side) I was commanding both the brigade and the regiment involved. Once when someone was asking me questions about the Jerusalem incident he said: "Who stopped it?" and I replied half in jest and without pausing to think: "I did," which, up to a point, I suppose, is true.

CHAPTER VI: ZERQA INTERLUDE

We returned to Zerqa in time for Christmas. Once more Allah was generous to us and prevented any of our drivers from planting their vehicles upside down in the Wadi Shaib — a feat which some of them were quite capable of executing.

It was good to see the whole Regiment on one parade ground again; and was a relief to find that their drill and turnout had not deteriorated while they were in the line. Every morning, unless the Regiment was on manoeuvres, I used to have a battalion drill parade at eight o'clock. This had various advantages. For one thing I enjoyed drilling them, but the main thing was that I could tell whether the company commanders were giving the men unauthorised leave, a practice which was formerly all too common in the Regiment. I had no objection to their giving men passes from after duty on Thursday to before duty on Saturday, but it was for Regimental Headquarters to decide if a man was to have leave at other times. The battalion parade usually lasted about an hour, and thereafter the companies carried on with their normal programme.

The Brigadier carried out an administrative inspection in January, 1955, when nothing very terrible happened, and we received visits from Glubb Pasha and General Cooke, each of whom reviewed the Regiment, and expressed themselves as being satisfied with what they saw. Later on General Sir Gerald Templer, then C.I.G.S. designate, who was visiting Jordan came to inspect the Regiment. After walking round the ranks he gave me a message for the men, saying that he wished them luck and adding "Tell them that in time of war I would rather have them on my side than against me!"

There was the usual routine work: confidential reports, cadres, courses, exercises, promotion examinations, and, of course, the Arab Legion Day Parade, for which Musayeb Suleiman once more trained our Guard of Honour to a high pitch of precision and smartness.

In Jordan the weekend falls on Thursday and Friday, and the weekly holiday was therefore from after duty on Thursday. The programme on that day was normally devoted to administrative matters, there would be a battalion parade, usually in best battle-dress, followed by the inspection of the barracks. Then in the hot weather most people adjourned to swim in the Zerqa Pool, a monument to the Transjordan Frontier Force.

Zerqa is not an earthly paradise, but it has two swimming baths, tennis and squash courts, a polo ground and several cinemas. Many of the quarters have well-established gardens and so, unless you happen to be particularly fond of the bright lights, there are worse places to soldier in. A pleasant way of spending a Friday was to take a picnic lunch and visit Ajlun or the crusader castle of Kerak, the ruined Byzantine city of Um el Jemal, or Jerash. Of these Jerash must take pride of place, and we visited it many times. The best way is to go by Amman and Sweilleh for the road is finished now and goes through much more attractive scenery than that of the Mafraq road. You pass the river Zerqa, the biblical Jabbok, at a place where the wadi is full of oleanders, and climb up into the edge of the Ajlun forest, green with pine trees. Then in a sharp angle of the road amongst olives in a deep valley stands the remains of a high broken wall of yellow stone, once the aqueduct of some flour mill. You pass the signpost that points to Ajlun and after a few more miles, rounding a corner the Bab Amman, a

Triumphal Arch dedicated to the Emperor Hadrian, who visited the city and wintered there in A.D. 129-30, is revealed. The arch, splendid at first glance, is sadly decayed.

We used to leave the car in the forum, and lunch in the shade of the wings of the South Theatre, which the Department of Antiquities have been restoring in recent years. A light railway has been installed for moving the massive stones: very useful for carrying the box with the lunch in it. The South Theatre could hold about four thousand people in its thirty-two tiers of seats, the lower rows of which are numbered in Greek, and so, it is supposed, could be reserved. It was built in the first century A.D. for a Greek inscription on the wall below the seats tells of a statue of Victory erected by a noncommissioned officer who served under Titus in the Jewish war of A.D. 70. It cost him three thousand drachmae, which sounds a lot of money for an N.C.O. to spend in such a way. The acoustics are still splendid, but for some reason when in 1955 the Amman Dramatic Society played *Julius Caesar* in Jerash, they chose to do it at the forum end of the main street. The forum is a peculiar shape, practically elliptical, but with its Ionic columns, golden in the sunlight, and unspoiled by any modern buildings it is impressive and attractive. Jerash has been lucky for it was unoccupied from mediaeval times until 1878, when the Turks settled a colony of Circassians there. Thus the place has not become the local quarry, and even the Circassian village only occupies a small area at the eastern end of the city.

Wandering northwards up the main street, the Street of the Columns, which has in recent years been cleared of debris and several feet of dirt, one can see the ruts cut by chariot wheels, and the round stone manholes which lead to the sewer below. The Roman bridge still stands, and so do some of the arches of the West Baths; temples to Zeus and Artemis, a cathedral; no day is long enough to see them all. The mosaic floor of the Church of Saints Cosmos and Damianus, enlivened with a variety of lifelike and enchanting animals, has been carefully restored. Theodore and Georgia paid for much of it between A.D. 529 and 533, and on the floor you may still see their portraits, among others which include Dagistheus, one of Justinian's generals.

Perhaps the most striking of all the monuments is the great Temple of Artemis, which, in crusader times when Jerash had long been uninhabited, was turned into a fort by the Atabey of Damascus, who garrisoned it with forty men. Despite the destruction wrought when it was captured by Baldwin II, King of Jerusalem (1118-31), it is still impressive, and it has a portico which can be seen from almost any part of the city, so commanding is its position.

Further up the valley, perhaps a mile away, lies a spring called Birkatein (the two cisterns), which supplies half Jerash with water. Beyond is the imposing tomb of a certain Germanus, and to the west, what must be the smallest of Roman theatres. The road is bad and the place remote, so that these ruins are seldom seen by the casual visitor, to his loss.

Jerash, or Gerasa, was one of the cities of the Decapolis, a league of free cities, to which Amman, the Roman Philadelphia, also belonged. Persians, Moslems and earthquakes all played their part in the decline of Jerash. It is said that the only trace of the former are goal-posts, erected in the Hippodrome beyond the South Gate for polo, where I have seen the Arabs playing football. For all the destruction and decay, Jerash is still the best preserved of the small Roman provincial cities in the Middle East. The place is seldom crowded with visitors; one walks among the ruins peopled only by a wild old Arab, who acts as watchman in the South

Theatre, his two picturesque if unwashed daughters who for a few piastres will allow tourists to photograph them, and a few boys, Arab or Circassian, who offer for sale little lamps or coins for the most part worn flat with age. It is not hard to people these empty streets with the Legions of former days.

In June we took over the Palace Guards once more. We were no longer responsible for Aqaba, but instead sent a company to Rutenberg in the Jordan Valley, not far South of the Sea of Galilee, a part of Jordan previously unknown to me. No. 3 Company found the majority of this guard, and as many officers were away on courses the detachment was commanded by Mansour Kreishan, the Signals Officer, and Abdulla Salim el Harbi, a recently joined cadet, who, though comparatively junior, proved steady and reliable.

At Rutenberg itself are the remains of a power-house dating from Mandate days, which was wantonly destroyed in 1948, and one of the major bridges over the Jordan — with an arch missing. A few miles to the South we had a strong guard at the Jisr-es-Sheikh Hussein, an iron bridge which looks as if it had been erected by the British Army in 1918. From the tower of the Police Post nearby one could see Israeli tractors at work two hundred yards away, but there was never any sign of guards.

North of Rutenberg I had another strong post above the Yarmuk near the point where Jordan, Syria and Israel join. From here one could look out towards the Sea of Galilee shimmering in the sunshine. A few miles away was the small town of Samakh, scene of a grim little fight on 25 September 1918, when the 4th Australian Light Horse, after charging the defences in the dark, cleared out the Turks and Germans by dismounted action.[8] Now the scene was perfectly peaceful; the

Israelis were watering the battlefield across which the Australians had galloped with artificial rain. Below us the Yarmuk, emerging from its gorge, meandered away to join the Jordan.

On 30th June His Majesty King Hussein, who had been on a visit to Europe, returned to Jordan, landing at Merka airfield. The Guard of Honour was mounted by 9 Regiment and commanded by Saoud Rashdan. The colour was on parade borne by Muhamad Rkheimeh, flanked by two battle-tried sergeants, Aitan Irdeini and Ma'an Ali. Addad Msayeh, wearing his Gallantry Medal, commanded the right half-company and Saoud Khaled, who though only a cadet was already a veteran, the left. Naqib Hleyil Mfadhi, resplendent in his red sash, and with an imposing row of medals on his chest, was the right-hand man. It was a good guard. The dun-coloured hills behind Merka and the light khaki drill of the soldiers, were brightened by the line of red shemaghs, the scarlet sashes, and the red, green and gold of the regimental colour.

As we waited for His Majesty's plane a noble-looking middle-aged Arab left a group of well-dressed bedouin and came towards me. In his dark-brown mantle trimmed with gold thread, and heavy white kaffiyeh, with neat beard and deeply lined face, he was a splendid figure.

"How is Jezzah?" he asked me: and it came to me that this was Abdel Kerim Irteimeh, a Belga Sheikh who lives near Merka. His son, Lance-Corporal Jezzah Abdel Kerim, was attached to the Regiment for experience as a section commander before going to the Cadet School. Many others of his tribe were in the Regiment and in the Jeish.

---

8 Colonel A. P. Wavell, C.M.G., M.C., *The Palestine Campaign*, p. 223.

As the plane, piloted by the King himself, landed, the guns drawn up behind the parade crashed out a royal salute. The aircraft taxied up in front of the Guard. A band played the National Anthem; the Guard presented arms and Rkheimeh dipped the colour in salute. Accompanied by Glubb Pasha and his A.D.C.s, the King inspected the Guard. He was returning it may be from a fateful tour, embracing as it did a visit to Paris, where the military attaché was Major Ali Abu Nawar, the present Chief of Jordanian Staff, who is credited with having organized the Young Officers' Movement, which was to play such a significant part early in the following year.

During most of June and July, the Brigadier being on his annual leave, I was temporarily in command of the Brigade. One of my tasks was to organize a demonstration for King Hussein showing how a battalion takes up a defensive position and the front which it can normally be expected to hold. As 9 Regiment were still on guard duties, 6 Regiment under Izzat Hassan staged the demonstration on the hills South of Khirbat es Samra, the next station North of Zerqa on the Hejaz railway. The country was open and so the battalion was well-deployed, the positions to be visited being wired. On the summit of the highest hill in the battalion's front line a tent was erected and from this viewpoint the audience could survey the whole scene. As the demonstration unrolled itself I had to give a commentary. The advanced guard of the enemy made contact, and fired Verey lights to indicate to their main body how far they had progressed; our guns brought down defensive fire — represented by a formidable array of made-up charges. 6 Regiment got down to details: prisoners were seen being marched in, their hands bound behind them.

Suleiman Ajaj, 9 Regiment's coffee-maker, appeared and after refreshing ourselves we descended to look round one of the forward positions, where infantry were dug in with a Charioteer, a 17-pounder and a section of Vickers. Then we inspected Izzat Hassan's headquarters, dug in and sandbagged. Afterwards His Majesty and the Defence Minister, who accompanied him, were shown round one of Jack Tirrell's batteries, dug in a few kilometres to the rear, and a casualty clearing point. The whole party, including Generals Glubb and Cooke, Brigadier Hutton and Colonel Luard, were afterwards invited to lunch at the Mess of the Divisional Signals.

But all that was only phase one of an elaborate operation. Phase two was a tour of the West Bank, when His Majesty was shown how it was proposed to defend the four hundred miles of frontier with the troops available. I was again involved in this, for it fell to me to explain the layout in the Northern Sector. I found it impossible to judge whether the King was convinced by what was being said, for although uniformly pleasant and polite, he seldom made any comment or asked any questions. We whirled round the area, a procession of big white cars and Land-Rovers, escorted by bedouin of the Pasha's bodyguard, down empty roads lined by policemen and gendarmerie. In the evening we slept in caravans on the rifle range at Hawara. The shelter behind the firing point was converted into a comfortable mess, the ante-room hung and carpeted with handsome oriental rugs, and rows of chairs were arranged in lines round the walls as is the Arab fashion, as if the ante-room were a chapter-house. Before dinner King Hussein sat here and talked to his officers. The conversation was mostly in English, at least until the arrival of Glubb Pasha, who seldom spoke to Arab officers except in their own tongue. Although His Majesty never entered into any conversation on purely military affairs, it was plain that his imagination was fired by any mention of the Air Force, and he would enter into the talk with animation, prepared to discuss the smallest details.

When the cortege moved on into Jerusalem district, I returned home. It is easy to be wise after the event, but I hope I will be believed when I say that I felt then that our efforts had been in vain. If we had convinced ourselves that we had the best plan of defence, we had not convinced the King. I do not think we need condemn ourselves for this, for I suspect that his mind was set against the plan before the presentation began — perhaps as recently as May 1955, in Paris.

The next and last demonstration which I had to organize for His Majesty was less controversial. It was simply a company attack, with support weapons, Vickers and mortars. This was carried out on the edge of the desert North-East of Khaw. The troops charged forward with great dash, and as none of them succeeded in walking into our mortar barrage, or getting his throat cut in any of the ways usual on such occasions, I think this one may be listed among our successes.

One of the "characters" of the Regiment was Sergeant Tobash Nahar. A Shammar from the Nejd, who joined the Legion in 1942, he won the Gallantry Medal in 1948, serving a 6-pounder anti-tank gun in 1 Regiment. A gun, with its shield all splashed with bullets, was in our anti-tank platoon in 1953, and Tobash alleged that this was the very piece, though nobody explained how it came to transfer itself to 9 Regiment. Tobash, who looked rather like a bedouin version of "Old Bill", was no fool, but he was distinctly idle; he was one of the best shots in the Regiment and, being a cunning old man, knew that he was too useful for us to be very beastly to him. His name, according to my interpreter, Ahmed Qasim, means "Break of Day". In the summer he married Joza, the daughter of

Corporal Saoud Eid, who was by all accounts a spirited woman. A black tent was put up in the space between the officers, and the other ranks' married quarters and the Shammar assembled to dance in honour of the occasion. The celebrations were held at night and many of the tribe, including retired soldiers and men of other regiments, came from Zerqa.

The dancers, twenty or thirty in number, draw up in two lines opposite each other, about fifteen yards apart, and join hands. Between them four men, including Abdulla Said the black M.T. Sergeant, beat time on shallow drums, which have clearly done duty at many weddings. The drum is suspended from the left elbow and beaten with a stick held in the right hand. Chanting, the ranks shuffle towards each other with short steps, bowing and lifting their heads in time to the drums. The tune, which seems to have only three notes and no words, is repeated endlessly, as the lines approach each other and retire, swaying to and fro, and gradually beginning to look more exalted, almost fey. Most of the dancers wear their civilian dress, but Muhamad Matar, Inad Nasir and a few others wear uniform. Some of the guests from Zerqa appear from their rich apparel to be people of some substance. The drums boom, the endless chant wavers up and down, and in the shadows around half the Regiment is watching. Salameh arrives and Khalaf Tlohi, a stout bedouin officer who is also attending the Staff College. Tea is brought, and in the black tent old Tobash, wearing a black mantle, and with a resigned look on his face, sits near the coffee pots. After a time a rival organization breaks into a Palestinian dance which they execute with more abandon than skill. Aitan Irdeini, his white teeth flashing, and Ali Salim lead the dance with Saoud Eid, the bride's father, who seems to be the only Shammar among them. One of the bedu, his shemagh wrapped round his head anyhow and hanging below his waist, like the hood of some mediaeval jester, trips up and down in front of them playing on a reed pipe.

The Shammar dance comes to an abrupt finish, amidst wild applause, while the dancers refresh themselves before throwing themselves once more into the fray. For a while the bogus Palestinians hold the floor.

The impromptu dance breaks up in confusion and once more the Shammar raise their monotonous, fascinating chant. The bearded drummer wheels about, strikes attitudes, draws forward first one line then the other, his drum throbbing as they advance.

When everyone else is exhausted Fuad Shahin, the Chief Clerk, a Moslem from Bethlehem, appears with his aoud, a sort of guitar, and sings the songs, mostly of Egyptian origin, which are now popular among the Arabs. I remember particularly one whose refrain went:

> Wen, ya Arab, wen, wen, wen?[9]
> Wen, ya Arab, wen, wen, wen?

which was much applauded by bedouin and haderi alike. It was a catchy tune.

The audience begins to thin out as midnight draws near, and we take our leave.

While the Brigadier was away I organized a Brigade Signals exercise in the mountains round Ajlun. Turki Hussein, who was rather good at this sort of thing, worked out the details of the exercise, and I occupied myself in visiting the three regiments, to see how they ran their headquarters. Suleiman

---

[9] Where, oh Arab, where, where, where?

Masoud, the commander of the Hashemite Regiment, told me that he had first come to the notice of Glubb Pasha when he had fought in these hills as a corporal during the troubles in 1939.

When the exercise ended I went to look at Ajlun Castle. Qala't-er-Rabad was built in 1184 by one of Saladin's amirs, and though destroyed by the Mongols in 1260, it was rebuilt shortly after by Sultan Baybars. Though now somewhat ruinous, it was occupied as late as the nineteenth century by Ibrahim Pasha. It is still strong for it has a deep moat hewn from the living rock and stands on a steep rounded hill. It is one large building having no courtyard; the roofs are still in a reasonable state and the towers, some of which are rather ruinous, have been sufficiently repaired to prevent further decay.

In August and September we had a series of brigade exercises, in the last of which we were supported by Major I. H. Mordecai-Jones' squadron of the Queen's Bays, which had come up from Ma'an. Their advent caused a great stir in the Regiment, for the men had never seen Centurions before. It was explained to the soldiers that none of these Inglezis knew a word of Arabic, and it was therefore up to them to learn English — and this they proceeded to do, at least sufficiently to indicate targets to the crews of the tanks. By the time we had done most section commanders knew "Right! Left! Up! Down!" and how to count up to ten. We were lucky in that we had about a week in which to practise various drills with this squadron before the manoeuvre in which, together, we burst out of a narrow valley, and went swarming across the plains South of the Mafraq — Irbid road, the bedouins, wildly excited, riding by platoons aboard the Centurions. *Wellah!* This was the way to go to battle. Why march?

On my journey to Aqaba in the summer of 1953 I had passed by the great crusader castle of Kerak in Moab. We had arrived in the dusk and had not stayed to explore it, but I was determined to return. It was not until one Friday in September two years later that we finally made this expedition by Land-Rover from Zerqa. The journey took about three hours. The going is good enough except for some thirty kilometres where it winds down into the Wadi el Mujib and up the other side by a road carved out of the cliff face.

Kerak of Moab was one of the fortresses built in the twelfth century, when Baldwin II and Fulk reigned as Kings of Jerusalem.[10] According to Toy[11] its date is about 1145, and it was in Latin occupation until 1188. It stands at the point of a land promontory, divided by a deep dry ditch from the walled town. South of the castle another moat cuts right across the promontory.

This was the fortress of Reynald de Châtillon, Prince of Antioch and Lord of Oultrejourdain, who was both brigand and pirate. His charming character is revealed in the following anecdote.

Requiring funds to organize an expedition to pillage Cyprus, he arrested the rich Patriarch of Antioch, who had displeased him, and flung him into prison, where he was cruelly beaten on the head. "His wounds were then smeared with honey, and he was left for a whole summer day chained in blazing sunshine on the roof of the citadel to be a prey for all the insects of the neighbourhood."[12] Funds now became available, and Reynald was able to ravage Cyprus to his heart's content. Detested by

---

[10] Runciman, III, 368.
[11] Toy, *History of Fortification*.
[12] Runciman, II, 347.

the Moslems, he was unlucky enough to be taken prisoner along with King Guy of Jerusalem after the battle of the Horns of Hattin. Saladin "seated the King next to him and, seeing his thirst, handed him a goblet of rose-water, iced with the snows of Hermon". Guy drank from it and handed it on to Reynald, who was at his side. By the laws of Arab hospitality to give food or drink to a captive meant that his life was safe; so Saladin said quickly to the interpreter: "Tell the King that he gave that man drink, not I,"[13] and himself beheaded Reynald with a sword, but the other prisoners were kindly treated. The incident is an interesting illustration of the importance which Arabs attach to the proper treatment of their guests.

After its capture the castle was refortified by the Moslems, who built the existing donjon in front of the old one, and added the outer wall on the West side. The entrance is on the North side, and fortunately the castle is kept locked so that it cannot be defaced or quarried. We found the key at the police post just North of the moat and were admitted without any difficulty. Kerak is probably not quite so impressive as the Krak des Chevaliers, but nevertheless with its thick walls and solid square towers it is still imposing. One of its most striking features is a number of vaulted underground chambers, which were evidently the barracks. There is accommodation for a very large garrison.

Kerak was the capital of a province and, besides the soldiers, had to house not only Reynald and his family but an administrative staff as well — clerks, tax-collectors, priests and so on. The keep, with the lord's residential quarters, still stands at the South corner of the enceinte, which, being furthest from the town, was presumably considered the most defensible position. Although much damaged, it was clearly a solid

---

[13] Runciman, II, 459.

building of the Norman style, with only one entrance. The larger rooms, though plain, were evidently large and airy, though no sign remains of any twelfth-century decoration. The outer wall on the West, built later by the Moslems, is very similar in style to the rest. The local National Guards now practise shooting in this bailey, where once their ancestors exercised with lance and bow.

Saladin besieged Kerak in November 1183, for while Reynald held it he was able to prey on the traffic between Syria and Egypt. It chanced that many nobles were met at Kerak to celebrate the marriage of Reynald's step-son, Humphrey of Toron, and the Princess Isabella. The small tower South-West of the Keep is still called "The Honeymoon Tower", for Saladin gallantly gave orders that the tower in which Humphrey and his young bride were lodged was not to be the target of his siege-engines.[14] The castle was relieved on this occasion by Baldwin IV, the leper King of Jerusalem.

Later, wishing to photograph the southern face, we decided to drive along the track which skirts the western wall. This was a mistake. It is the merest donkey path and runs along the edge of a precipice. In width it seemed to me to be at least two inches narrower than the Land-Rover, but once embarked on this perilous journey there was no going back, for there was no place to turn until we reached the South moat. Halfway along we encountered a heavy-blooded gang of labourers, who appeared to be engaged in destroying what little surface remained, and who were in no hurry to get out of the way. Needless to say, having finally reached the South moat and taken our photographs, with trembling hands, we had to return by the same route.

---

[14] Runciman, II, 441.

At the end of October it was announced that General Bayar, the President of Turkey, had been invited to make a state visit to Amman. The King of Jordan had visited Ankara and naturally wished to return this hospitality. At the same time it was felt that there was a very grave security risk involved, for the Turks, who had long ruled in Palestine and Transjordan until ousted in 1918, were not remembered with affection by the Arabs. 2 Brigade was to be responsible for internal security in Amman during the visit, and the Brigadier detailed me to organize a series of demonstrations to show the Brigade how to deal with rioters. Streets were taped out in our camp and Sukheil Hammad and the Vickers Platoon played the part of the riot squad. Nos. 1 and 2 Companies were detailed as demonstrators. This was just the sort of role that appealed to the jundis, who came surging out from between two barrack rooms, the ponderous form of Nazzal Hleyil waving his shemagh and gallumphing in the van. 1 Company advanced with cries of "Muhamad Moazi minshan Barlaman!" and "Khurrb el hukumat Younq Bey!" which being translated means "Muhamad Moazi for Parliament" and "Down with the Government of Young Bey." Adding the title "Bey" was a nice touch, I thought. When Nazzal raised his stick the mob halted smartly and shut its collective trap, so that Sukheil could warn the populace that if they did not disperse he would charge. The Vickers Platoon, shemaghs wrapped over faces, fixed bayonets and looked menacing. Well, as you guessed, the mob did not disperse, but instead advanced ten paces. Sukheil now led forward his men, and when Nazzal once more held up his stick the mob faced to the rear and galloped off, realistically pursued with butt and bayonet. As usual in amateur productions, though the play was good, the really funny part was the rehearsals.

on the pavement, and not rush into the ranks to take their pictures as was their custom. The shadows lengthened but eventually General Bayar, an old gentleman in a top hat and morning coat, drove up and alighted at the gate of the Palace. As he inspected the Guard, Madhat, carried away with enthusiasm, dashed into the road, and knelt before the advancing President to snap him as he passed the colours; it was with difficulty that I prevented his colleagues from following his example.

One night there was a party at the Turkish Embassy. I had the whole of 2 Company under Nazzal Hleyil drawn up round the building, at intervals of a few paces and the Vickers platoon on guard within. After inspecting the soldiers, I went into the garden and watched the visitors arriving. After a time I was joined by an Arab Colonel who sat talking to me for a long time. It was now that I heard the name of Ali Abu Nawar for the first time. He was a major and the military attaché in Paris, and it seemed that he was coming home to be Chief A.D.C. I got the impression that my companion thought this an unsuitable appointment.

The weather did not break until the last day of our stay in Amman. We had had a full week, for although there had been no disturbances there were the usual alarums, and the consequent changes of dispositions.

Amman is a city of steep hills and narrow valleys. The streets on the high ground were constantly patrolled so that we would have early warning of any gathering. The schools were closely watched, and, as two years earlier, we reinforced the main police station with a platoon. Most of the Regiment was concentrated, but much time was taken up in visiting the isolated platoons and patrols. After a time as our area was quiet, we had to take over the area near the Philadelphia Hotel, and I put Hammad Faleh and 4 Company into the Municipal buildings. He was to patrol the hillside opposite the palace, where Ahmed Sudqi Pasha lived.

The streets were already wet and slushy as the Regiment drove away to Khaw, and the sky told of more rains to come. I stood on the side of Jebel Amman watching the trucks moving off below me. Pigeons wheeled round the white minaret of a mosque pencilled against the leaden sky. This was the end of a chapter for we were now due to return to Palestine. Amman was quiet, and the Grand Turk had gone off with a whole skin. Perhaps Qiada had overestimated the dangers of trouble during his stay. More likely the sight of a whole brigade ready beforehand had discouraged would-be troublemakers.

All seemed well, but had we known it only four months remained....

CHAPTER VII: THE DECEMBER RIOTS

As soon as the President of Turkey had safely quitted Amman we began to press forward our arrangements for the move to Palestine. The actual journey of the Regiment presented no great difficulty, but reconnaissance of the new area was bound to take time.

When we were in Jerusalem in 1954 the Regiment had been concentrated; our new sector in the North was very different, stretching from East of Jenin to within a few miles of Tulkarm it included much of ancient Samaria. The Arab Legion is deployed along a four hundred mile front and has a dual role: to guard against Israeli aggression, and to prevent Arab infiltrators stealing across the border and causing incidents in Israel. Hardly a night goes by without some hapless Palestinian falling into the hands of his compatriots. Israeli aggression had already included big raids on the Qibya pattern and small ones on the Azzoun model. The dispositions appropriate to meet raiding operations were not necessarily those best calculated to repel a major invasion.

Allenby had taken Jerusalem in December 1917, but it was not likely that the Israelis would choose to strike during the rainy season, and so our initial dispositions were designed to prevent infiltration. Mobile reserves were grouped ready to reinforce the frontier villages, which were held by their own National Guards, sometimes assisted by police cavalry, and sometimes by a section or a platoon of regulars.

It will be recalled that the Arab Legion had, at this time, only three infantry brigades, but ever since Qibya the equivalent of two had been required on the West Bank. Brigades were relieved annually, so that they could train and refit, and since there was no Fourth Infantry Brigade we found ourselves taking over from an ad hoc formation, drawn from the 2nd Armoured Cars and a National Guard regiment. Strickland, the commander, was suffering from an old wound, and I was taken round by his Intelligence Officer, a young bedouin, and by Said Saleh, my own I.O. who being from Deir Ghazaleh near Tulkarm, knew the area very well.

Said Saleh, a haderi second lieutenant, practically defies description. Stout, jolly, loyal, deceitful, stupid — I cannot find words to do him justice. In 1948 he commanded some irregulars in the Palestine War. They numbered, as he assured me once, some three thousand. A great gardener, he was not afraid of hard work, and did much to improve our barracks at Khaw by caring for the trees, flower-beds and buildings. He was a great friend of Saoud Rashdan, who was never one to favour gloomy people. Although much given to lying and boasting, usually to bolster up his own morale or to avoid correction, Said Saleh accepted every rebuke in good part, and was an asset if only because it was practically impossible to offend him. He used to complain that I gave him a rocket every day for his breakfast.

Travelling in Land-Rovers we visited most of the frontier posts. The efficiency and smartness of the National Guard regiment which came from Tubas, Tayasir and the surrounding villages, was most striking. One lance-corporal, who was acting as a platoon sergeant had actually held the latter rank in the Transjordan Frontier Force and had been an instructor. The post was under a rather wet cadet, and I had no illusions as to who really commanded the platoon. These men had been called up for about eight months, and although they were only paid five Jordan Dinars a month they really enjoyed serving, and were probably better off financially than they would have been at home. The Arab, whether bedouin or fellahin, still feels that it is a privilege to carry arms. With the bedouin it is merely that he considers raiding or soldiering to be the only occupation worthy of a man. With the Palestinian peasant the motive is self-preservation, the desire to defend their lands from the fate of Jaffa, Nazareth and Acre. We were now in an area where rebellion had been hottest in 1936-39 and the regiment I was visiting was from the very heart of the region which had been in revolt. There had been several incidents in my district during the time it was held by the armoured car regiments.

I set up my headquarters in a Teggart fort, built by the Palestine Police and capable of holding about one hundred men, besides offices, the officers' mess, stores and the Medical Inspection room. The soldiers, who were not accommodated within lived in tents inside the wire which surrounded the place. A young doctor, Urfan Johari from Nablus, was now attached to the Regiment. Educated at the University of Beirut he was serving for a time in the Legion to save money for his further education. He was a great asset for he got on well with the bedouin, and although he had no military experience was anxious to learn and to help. Almost the first night in our new headquarters the big dark tent allotted to the sick blew down. There were usually several patients, who were not sufficiently ill to be evacuated and finding the tent so unsatisfactory we cleared one of the rooms in the police fort, and organized a small hospital where they could recuperate in comparative comfort.

There was in the fort a detachment of nine mounted policemen, under a waqil; they did not seem to resent our invasion and were very co-operative. They usually had to put up with soldiers in their barracks, and these at least tidied the place up, and arranged for the numerous broken windows and doors to be repaired, so that when Nadeem Bey, their colonel, descended upon them they were able to show him how diligently they looked after their fort, and everybody was happy. There were cells near the main door of the post, which were seldom unoccupied, and the cavalrymen spent long hours in the saddle patrolling the villages in the area. They certainly inspired more confidence than the police infantry and were a better class of man, for each brought his own horse on first joining.

The main body of 9 Regiment was spread around the district in tented camps, police forts or hired houses in the frontier villages. Detachments varied from a company with the 3-inch mortar platoon under command, to a section on its own. My days seemed to be spent in the Land-Rover. After perhaps half an hour in the office I would drive out to one of the outlying companies to visit the platoons on detachment, to walk along the demarcation line and to get to know the lay of the land in case we should find ourselves with a hot war on our hands. I wanted to know every road and every track by which the Israelis could possibly drive into the area; and every place where there was no track, but where the map seemed to indicate a possible run. Once one of these trips ended with the Land-Rover hopelessly bogged in the middle of the plain that lies between Jenin and Ya'abad; another time Juma'a drove us across the watershed between Sanur and Ain Fara. When they were not shoving from behind, Abdulla Heikal and Hamed Inad had to run ahead clearing away the boulders.

At one time there was a detachment at Bardala, South of Beisan, and after visiting a battalion exercise, which Captain

Fendi Omeish of 6 Regiment was running for the National Guard near Jiftlik, I decided to go and have a look at my platoon. On the way we stopped in a wadi, and setting up some rocks as targets, practised for a while with our stens and lugers. We came eventually, to our surprise and disgust, to a pass where, though nobody had bothered to mention it, there was a deep and wide anti-tank ditch in the road, with numerous dragons' teeth blocking the wadi alongside. We had come a long way and had no intention of going back: a Land-Rover is a remarkable machine, and after one or two false casts and half an hour wasted we reached the top of an apparently impassable hill to the West, and managed with much reconnoitring to find a slope gentle enough to lead us down the other side.

The Vickers platoon was at Bardala under Corporal Muhamad Matar, a great talker. Though unexpected and unannounced, we came in a blessed hour, and were pressed to take lunch. We sat on the iron bedsteads and drank endless glasses of tea, without milk but with plenty of sugar and mint. It was a very hot day, and as we were already in winter dress, we were driven to change into shirt-sleeve order. We visited the mukhtar, looked at the weapons of the National Guard and discussed their problems, before visiting our patrol, prowling the frontier and watching towards Beisan. The Israeli sentry could be plainly seen on a nearby hill. Beyond, a tractor was at work. Then in the evening we turned home, and following the Wadi Malih drove up the valley which leads to Tayasir. We passed the hot springs where an ancient bath stands in the shade of tall trees. In the morning we had seen an old man whose plough was drawn by a camel tilling the soil in the Jordan valley. Now we passed a man in a blue gallabiya riding home on a rough-looking grey country-bred horse, his wooden plough across his saddle bows. The rough road wandered up into the mountains, overlooked everywhere by rugged hills, and once by the ruins of a deserted tower. We came to the edge of Tayasir, solid grey stone houses among olives and vivid green fields on a plateau between trackless mountains. Here at the well two little girls were drawing water. One was dark and dressed in black, the other wore a faded red dress, and her hair which fell to her shoulders was as fair as that of a nordic child. When the soldiers went to drink from their black leather bucket they hardly dared to speak for shyness, so rarely do these villagers see strangers. We drove on through Tubas and Ain Fara back to the main road along the precipitous sides of the gorge leading to Askar and Nablus, the road where British aircraft smote the retreating Turks in 1918.

So we spent our days. Sometimes the men would be repairing the roads to a frontier village; or digging trenches to cover some pass; wiring an outpost or practising the action to be taken if ambushed on the way to an incident. The days were never the same and never dull, the men were happy in this work, and November passed all too soon.

Not a night went by that we did not set nearly fifty ambushes, some mixed, consisting of National Guardsmen as well as regulars or policemen, some entirely bedouin. It was not impossible that National Guardsmen should be in league with infiltrators from their own village, and for that reason I preferred patrols of my own men.

Some villages liked having soldiers in them; others did not. One suspected that the last category had a profitable line in smuggling. Faqqua' in the north was one of the villages that welcomed and co-operated with its garrison, perhaps because there had been a shooting match there a few months earlier. During this incident the villagers had nearly succeeded in shooting Ray Leakey, the commander of 1st Armoured Car Regiment, who, while trying to stop the firing, had got between the Arabs and the Israelis. They were still deeply embarrassed when reminded of it. Anin, a village on our Western front, certainly did not like to be garrisoned, although it was completely overlooked by a mountain in Israeli territory a little to the West. When 2nd Armoured Car Regiment put some men there the villagers succeeded in getting them withdrawn by complaining that the jundis had tried to get off with their women. This smelt like a put up job. Some time before we arrived there had been an incident near the village when a patrol had killed a smuggler and taken several others, and it was evident that this country, of steep wadis and olive groves, was a likely area for running cattle into Israel where they commanded a high price. One of my earliest visits was to Anin where I went ostensibly to inspect the defences, and the demarcation line. The mukhtar, a fat, sly, jolly man and the regular corporal in charge of the defences, a keen and alert bedu from 3 Regiment, accompanied me. We climbed up the hill, looked at the wire, inspected the new school beyond and arranged to provide pickets to guard the people when they ploughed near the frontier. We lunched at the house of the mukhtar, who was clearly much influenced by a tall, cleanshaven, bent old man with a dark brown kaffiyeh, who seemed to be his familiar. I suggested that they would like reinforcement.

"*Wellahi*, there is no fear. There is no danger here."

"But the patrols, the world night, after a time your National Guards will become tired from them."

"All is their duty."

The eyes twinkled in his round and oddly boyish face, for he felt he had got the better of this exchange. For a time I let the matter rest, but it was not long before we received strict orders to make measures against infiltration our Number One Priority. I thought once more of Anin, and suggested that the mukhtar should be invited to place an empty house at our disposal so that we could billet a section there. Curiously enough there was not so much as a vacant room in the whole village. To the disgust of the villagers we managed to produce two brand new 180-pounder tents, and Sergeant Saad Saoud with a section to live in them. It was mentioned that the story of the soldiers who trifled with the local girls was already known to us — and disbelieved. Driving into the police post at Jenin one day I noticed the smiling mukhtar and his gloomy white-faced friend among the crowd of suppliants outside the office of the local police officer. I cannot say what the object of their visit may have been, but when I left the district a section of 3 Company still dwelt in their midst.

Soon after our arrival on the West Bank we were told to redouble our precautions against infiltration. The Egyptians, finding that the situation in the Gaza area was becoming too touchy for their taste, were trying to distract the Israelis by stirring up trouble on the Jordanian front. Refugees were being bribed to cross the border at night and carry out small raids.

On the night of 20/21st November an Israeli truck was shot up near Lajjun a few miles from the North-West corner of our area. Next morning the Mixed Armistice Commission held an investigation, but there was very little evidence to show who was to blame. Jordan was not condemned. After the investigation Brigadier Green conferred with me and Colonel Nadeem Saman, the commander of Nablus Police District. Nadeem evidently suspected that the people of Rummaneh village had had a hand in this affair. The mukhtar, Fayar Darweesh, was arrested and taken to Jenin.

Rummaneh, a village of just over a thousand inhabitants of whom more than six hundred are refugees receiving U.N.R.W. A. rations, lost half its land when the truce-line was laid down at the Rhodes Conference in April 1949. The people of Rummaneh are the more bitter because at the end of the fighting Arab troops were many kilometres West of the village. Many square miles of land which had been theirs from time immemorial had to be given up to people who had not even won it by right of conquest. They do not understand it. And nor do I.

There were police in the village, and the National Guards were commanded by a regular N.C.O.: if the raid had really been launched from here it looked as if these people, bribed perhaps, were not taking their duties very seriously. I proposed sending a section to live in the village, and the Brigadier agreed. Dakheel Juma'a, a Howeiti N.C.O. from 2 Company, was selected for the job; a tall rugged bedouin of about thirty, he was a severe and imposing sergeant who would stand no nonsense from the fellahin. At the same time I told Said Saleh, the intelligence officer, to get busy and find out what had been going on. On the 23rd Said, accompanied by two of the intelligence section, Mahmoud es Shobeki and Suleiman Ayadeh, spent most of the day sniffing around Rummaneh, returning to report that before the incident the raiders had conferred in the house of Ahmed el Faleh, and that those present included Mahmoud el Haj Rarib of Rummaneh and Mustafa al Asmar of Taiyibeh, the next village; the latter had been a dashing leader in the Palestine rebellion of 1936. Abu Brahim es Srir of Acre, one of Haj Ameen's men, used to come down from Syria each month with money to pay the raiders.

This was all very fine so far as it went, and we passed it on to Brigade and to the police. I thought I would have a look at Said Saleh's informant and a meeting was arranged in an olive grove between Rummaneh and Zebouba. It was a bright windy morning and Said took some time to produce his spy, a man of repellant aspect who inspired no confidence whatever. Our conference produced no further information, although he spent some time repeating what we already knew. I told him to let us know if he ever got wind that Abu Brahim was back in the area, not that I thought he was likely to come while we had a section in the village.

There was no other serious incident of this sort during the time I was in the Jenin area. Generally speaking infiltrators were more innocent in their intent. Smuggling may be their object, but more often they go to take oranges from a grove which was once their own or to visit relatives living beyond the wire in some divided village. The genius who laid down the armistice line thought nothing of dividing a house from its garden; or a village from its well. There is one village where the boys' school is in Israel and the girls' school in Jordan; sometimes a man can pick the dates from one side of his tree but not the other. The line was laid down far away in Rhodes, apparently with the aid of small-scale maps and strong drink.

Here are two typical examples of minor infiltration which took place when we were in North Palestine.

At about 4 p.m. on 15th December, Hamed Abdel Kader Muhamad Hreish and Farhan Hassan Hreish of Nazareth left the village of Sandala in the Israeli-occupied territory and crossed the frontier near Deir Ghazaleh. Moathib Salim, a very alert and active cadet, who was commanding the platoon there, went out with two of his men and captured them. They were taken to Jenin and handed over to the police. One of them had two gold sovereigns on him. Both said that their only object was to come and live in an Arab country.

On another occasion a diligent Hejazi Corporal, Muhamad Faleh of the 17-pounder platoon, with a mixed patrol caught a man who was trying to get across the Jenin-Ta'anik road and infiltrate into Israel. He had been released from prison a week before, and was trying to get back to Acre district, which was his home. One could hardly help feeling a little sorry for him.

During his visit it seems that General Bayar wasted little time in broaching the question of the Baghdad Pact,[15] and the possibility of Jordan becoming a member. The Government of Said el Mufti not unnaturally wished to know what material advantages this might have for the Hashemite Kingdom, and dropped a hint that the Arab Legion would be none the worse for a few extra formations. The Turks replied that their resources were limited, and were barely sufficient to keep up their own army of twenty-five divisions. They suggested that Jordan should approach Her Majesty's Government on the subject, since Great Britain was already her ally and subsidised the Legion. In due course a letter was written detailing the formations and units with which it was hoped to increase the Jeish. This document, perhaps to the surprise of the Jordan Government, was well received by H.M.G. who seem to have raised no objections, but sent the C.I.G.S. to discuss details.

Between the visits of Generals Bayer and Templer, General Hakim Amer of the Egyptian Army visited Jordan, intent no doubt on undoing any harm that the Turks might have done.

The first few days of General Templer's visit passed peacefully in Nablus district, and it was taken for granted that

---

[15] A defensive alliance signed between Iraq and Turkey in February, 1955, to which Iran, Pakistan and the U.K. have subsequently acceded.

the Pact was as good as signed. This was very satisfactory as it meant that the Jeish would get the fourth infantry brigade, which it so badly needed, and a regiment of medium artillery, not to mention planes and tanks. But the days passed and the negotiations were not concluded. Each morning as we drove to work Ahmed Qasim would tell me that he had heard on the wireless that the General's departure had been postponed for another twenty-four hours. Then on 17th December, as we were passing through Silat ed Dahr we were halted by a crude road-block made of stones and boulders. The local schoolboys were there in force shouting and throwing stones, the chief offender was a lad in khaki shorts. "After him! Whatever you do get that one!" Seeing the soldiers dismount the boys ran off in all directions, but Juma'a and Hamed Inad sprinted after the ringleader and cornered him by the Post Office. When I arrived Juma'a was standing on him. Considerably shaken he was secured in the Land-Rover. I rounded up some of the men of the village, told them to see that the road was cleared and drove off. Our captive was handed over to the police. The waqil was away, but the lance-corporal was a good, keen man, and as soon as he heard what was going on he saddled his horse and rode off to the village. I told Khdayer and Salim Hussein to take a truckload of soldiers, and to make sure that the villagers cleared the road as ordered.

I spent a short time in the office and then drove back to see that all was quiet. On the way we met some of the boys from outlying villages, such as El Fandagoumiye, going home. They said there was no school that day. Soon after I arrived at Silat ed Dahr a procession came down the hill from the South. It was the schoolboys of Burqa village, who had marched five miles to make a demonstration. They hesitated when they saw the soldiers, but then came on once more. Several of them spoke English.

"We want Freedom," they cried, making no attempt to explain what they wanted freedom from. One of them said that one of the soldiers had hit him.

"Why does he hit me?" he said.

"Perhaps he does not like you."

I asked them whether they would not like to go home, and said I would provide transport. The younger children who were footsore thought this was a very good idea indeed. The older youths thought it was a wicked plot to trap them and take them to prison. Without much trouble we persuaded them that it was a genuine offer, and that got rid of them. They had behaved perfectly well, but it was astonishing that they should have thought it worthwhile to stump all the way from Burqa to so little purpose. They were clearly pretty excited about the Pact, and it was quite obvious that the schoolmasters were at the bottom of it. I assembled the Mukhtar, the elders of Silat and the teachers in a room next the Post Office. I told them that I blamed them, and that I was not going to have the roads blocked in my area; that the bedouin were rough and might hurt them, and that if I had any more trouble I would put *them* inside. I was responsible for the defence of their area, and I was not prepared to let them block roads by which I might have to move reinforcements to the frontier villages. I talked to them of the part which the Regiment had played in Jerusalem and pointed out that the soldiers were their brethren, and were on their side. If they attacked or hindered us it was the Israelis who would benefit. I then allowed myself to be persuaded to release our captive, and after drinking coffee together, we went our several ways, fairly friendly. We had no further trouble in Silat ed Dahr.

The 19th was lively. It chanced that I was to visit Brigade Headquarters that morning to go through my officers' annual confidential reports with the Zaim. We had not been long engaged in this task when the telephone rang: it was Joan. She said that a crowd was attacking the house of the British Vice-Consul, and she thought we might like to know. Jackie Hackett-Payne, a retired Major of the Queens, was our next-door neighbour, and had lived in Rafidia for about fourteen years. His Arab friends were legion and he had never previously been the object of any attack. A crowd which was said to have numbered several thousands, marched out of Nablus, and several hundred, mostly school-children, attacked the Vice-Consulate, while a large mob stood in the field opposite, where there is a high bank, from which vantage point they stoned the house. There was a section of police infantry stationed in a post across the road, but they did nothing, even failing to tell Brigade Headquarters what was going on. It is suspected that they concealed themselves behind the Vice-Consulate. Some of the larger boys climbed on to the garden wall and hacked down the British coat of arms which hung over the gate. A great cheer went up as it fell to the ground. The crowd now burst open the gate and poured into the front garden, trampling the flowers and wrecking the beds. A man climbed up and tore down the Union Jack, which floated over one corner of the building. Elias Salfiti, Hackett-Payne's chief clerk, was the hero of the hour, for although hit on the head by a stone during the struggle, he succeeded in wresting the flag from the man who had lowered it, and eventually persuaded the crowd to disperse.

The Brigadier sent a section from Brigade Headquarters to guard the Vice-Consulate, and I left for Nablus, reaching Rafidia by a back street South of the town, which is sometimes clear in times of disorder. The Brigadier had ordered me to put a guard at the Vice-Consulate, and I spoke to Khdayer, who detailed a section from 4 Company, to go and relieve the men from Brigade. I then called on Hackett-Payne, who described without heat what had occurred, and defended the wretched corporal in charge of the police, who, he said, had done all he could. I told the corporal that in my opinion an old woman would have done about twice as well.

After these delays I set off for my headquarters. We had not reached Deir Sheraf when we saw a bus coming towards us, bulging with excited Arabs shouting and waving banners. We managed to stop it. An earnest little man jumped off and said that they were on their way to Nablus to demonstrate.

Again they raised their familiar and meaningless cry of "We want Freedom! We want Freedom!"

I asked where they came from, and was surprised to find that they were our friends of yesterday from Burqa, but this time the grown men were there as well. I suggested that they should go home, but they said that would bring shame on them, as two more busloads with the rest of the villagers had preceded them. I toyed with the idea of taking their ignition key, but since they were not committing any offence I decided to let them alone. They were all very friendly and cheerful, and with more cries of "We want Freedom" from them, we went our respective ways.

On arriving at R.H.Q. I was told by Fuad that there was a demonstration in Jenin, where Musayeb was in charge. No details were known, and so I decided to go and see what was happening. Khdayer insisted on coming as well, and followed in his Land-Rover with Salim Hussein, the R.S.M.

There was a mob of perhaps a thousand people at the crossroads in the middle of Jenin, standing outside the municipal buildings. They were not doing anything and we drove through without incident. Musayeb had No. 1 Company ready to move, but concealed within the courtyard, where the inhabitants could not see them. I wanted to see the Chief of Police, but he was in the town where the crowd, which had increased, was a little restive. People were climbing up the stairs into the Town Hall and forcing their way on to the balcony. Every now and then someone would come to the front of the balcony and address those in the street below. I pushed my way through the people and up the stairs, and met the police commander, who though he had not shaved, seemed otherwise much as usual. He did not want to call out the troops. The mayor was inside the building and presently began to read out an announcement which the Government had issued and which was relayed to the assembled populace. The policeman and I went in and joined him, and Khdayer followed. A number of notables were sitting with him. People from the balcony kept shoving into the room. After he had spoken for a few minutes the mayor was called to the telephone in an adjoining room. Some of the people tried to follow him, but this we prevented. He returned and finished his speech, being followed by a tall, youngish Imam with a full beard, and a fine bass voice. When they had done we succeeded in clearing the onlookers from the building, and went on to the balcony again. This also we gradually cleared, though some people still hung about in the street below. Soon these also began to disperse, and in Jenin at least no heads had been broken. I heard later that the people there thought I was a Circassian.

Jenin was barely a mile behind us when we saw a crowd of people, mostly schoolboys, going towards the town. It seemed to me that it would be a pity to permit this when things were just settling down and that without calling the troops out. We halted two youths who were some way ahead of the rest. They said that they came from Qabatiya, and they looked to me like junior school teachers. Of course, if they wanted to go to Jenin I really had no right or authority to stop them, but they were clearly uncertain of themselves, for they stopped and stood by the roadside after they had gone a little way past us. Their followers, probably their pupils, approached and we shouted at them to go back home; they hesitated, and I began to rattle my stick on the asphalt of the road. I was carrying a long bamboo such as bedouin camelry use. The youth of Qabatiya did not care for the look of this weapon, and most of them took off for home at a good pace. Some of them had been trotting along barefoot, and only stopped to put on their shoes. One or two tried to slip past us but without success. We followed up this rabble, and speeded them on their way.

It was getting late as we drove towards R.H.Q., and Juma'a tried to break through the sound barrier. Swinging round a corner we came on a well-sited road block, which was still under construction — just as well, for we only managed to pull up about forty yards beyond. About half a dozen lads who had been building this obstacle, took to the fields; five were soon rounded up, but the sixth was well away and going strong. I pulled out my luger and fired a shot in the air. He was simple enough to stop and give himself up. We set these knaves to work to clear the road, and asked them where they came from. They said that they were from Arraba, had been given a holiday from school, and had been told by some of the older boys to go out and block the Jenin road. We took their names. I doubted whether these particular youths would again offend, and suggesting that they should inform their seniors and teachers what trouble they had been in, we told them to run home, and not to stop running until they got there. They did.

There was a minor demonstration in Ya'abad, but this dispersed peaceably, and that was the extent of the trouble in my sector. Other commanders were not so fortunate.

In Amman there was some shooting. Jan Bradford, the C.O. of 1 Regiment, was hit on the head by a stone, and fell to the ground stunned. As he came to he heard a splutter of musketry from his soldiers, who being bedouin, were not prepared to permit such liberties. The windows of Legion vehicles were smashed by stones, and cars were turned over. In breaking up the mobs gas bombs were used for the first time in Jordan. The casualties were estimated at one killed and seven wounded; a few policemen got broken heads. Beyond question the riots were serious and well organized, and when they were over the King and the Pasha went round together thanking the troops who had restored order. A Christian Arab lieutenant-colonel, who was a warm supporter of the Chief of the General Staff, said at the time, "If nothing else has resulted, at least these riots have brought the King and the Pasha closer together."

In Jerusalem there had been serious rioting. The police opened Herod's Gate and loosed the mob from the Old City. Pat Gray, at the head of a section of 3 Regiment, charged, drove them back and got the gate shut again. He gave the police a direct order to keep it shut, but no sooner had he turned his back than they re-opened it and the mob poured out and made for the Turkish Consulate in Sheikh Jerrah, which they proceeded to set on fire. Once more Pat Gray charged, this time at the head of a bunch of soldiers from 5 Regiment, who were none to eager for the fray. On this occasion he also was hit on the head by a stone. A small girl was trampled to death by the mob; a false and malicious rumour was circulated that another girl who was lighting paraffin to set the consulate aflame had been shot by an Inglezi. Both these young ladies, of course, became martyrs! I was amazed at such an outbreak in Jerusalem, which had been so peaceful a year earlier.

In Bethlehem, normally the quietest of towns, there was serious rioting, and several people were shot by the police. A family, one of whose members had been hanged for espionage, were thought to be among the ringleaders.

Said el Mufti, as a Circassian and the head of a minority, did not care to bring the hatred of the Arabs on his community, and resigned, being replaced by Haza'a Majali of Kerak. The 19th December found us still waiting for this new Government to join the Baghdad Pact, but this was not to be, for the West Bank members of the Cabinet managed to prevent it. At this time the Arabs of Palestine were strongly pro-Nasser, so much so that whenever his picture appeared in the cinema the audience would clap; his picture was often carried in processions during the demonstrations. The West Bank, which takes its political information chiefly from the Egyptian broadcast "Voice of Arabia", was dead against any line-up with Turkey, Iraq or Britain, as opposed to Egypt. Amman itself is full of Palestinian refugees, and they, together with school-children inflamed by their teachers who in many cases were Egyptians, had turned demonstrations into riots. When such pressure can force a Prime Minister into resignation it is mob rule, nothing less. Whenever the genuine opponents of the Government promised to behave, as they did in Nablus, the Communists took care to start something and thus to bring more moderate leaders into disrepute.

In Jericho the object of the rioters appears to have been pillage rather than any political end. The refugees rioted and burnt an U.N.R.W.A. store, but not before they had taken the precaution of removing its contents. Women were seen making off for the camps with sacks and bundles on their heads, labour which the men could hardly be expected to perform. The chicken and turkey farm belonging to Moussa Alami, who employed many refugees, was looted and wrecked, years of work on improving the stock being thrown away in a few hours.

In Hebron it is said that refugees managed to burn the whole of their winter supply of paraffin.

In Tulkarm a Land-Rover belonging to 6 Regiment was burnt, and in Nablus an armoured car was damaged and members of the crew were injured. I was surprised to hear the squadron commander, Abdulla Qa'ad, commend the corporal for being "somewhat wise" and offering no resistance.

The Arab Legion came through these days of mob rule with credit. The Army did not seem to be in any real doubt as to the benefits of joining the Baghdad Pact, and even such unreliable elements as the Signals seemed to have only a few troublemakers in their ranks. The bedouin as ever were solidly behind anything that the Pasha approved. In 9 Regiment this was so much the case that it was hardly necessary to lecture the men and tell them what the Pact was for. It was thought that His Majesty King Hussein was himself strongly in favour of the alliance.

For my own part I viewed with distrust the Jordanian education system, nor did I believe the country was much better for its elections or its Parliament. I believed in having plenty of soldiers on hand before anything happened, and hitting somebody quite hard when it did happen. But this was precisely what the Government had not done. The mob had achieved its aim; by bringing sufficient pressure to bear it had prevented successive Prime Ministers from joining the Baghdad Pact.

Complete calm followed the storm and at least in so far as the Nablus sector was concerned everything returned to normal with uncanny speed. The riots were switched on and then switched off again, it seemed as simple as that.

I returned to my normal round, visits to the outposts, tactical exercises without troops for the National Guard, walks along the demarcation line, and long hours ploughing through the men's annual reports: thus my days were spent.

Christmas 1955 came in peace, and we drove down to Jerusalem and attended the service in St. Georges. An old friend, Pat Leonard, now Bishop of Thetford, preached the sermon, and was able to break the programme of his pilgrimage to spend a few hours with us next day. An ominous portent attended the close of this service, for within a few minutes the skies grew dark and thunder crashed out over the Holy City. Lightning struck down the summit of one of the pinnacles of the Cathedral. A thunderstorm on Christmas Day, and one which smote the Church of St. George, could hardly be interpreted as a good omen.

Visiting Baga esh Shargiyye, unannounced, I found Salameh Haza'a, now a corporal, commanding a section in the Police Post. Everything was in good order, and the men turned out as if for a ceremonial parade. I felt faintly surprised, and certainly gratified. Moreover, the Police Sergeant spoke warmly of the conduct of the men, who were diligent and helpful. I felt they had whitened my face. I was sure that my visit was unexpected, as I had only decided to go to Baga on the spur of the moment. Salameh Haza'a was no more efficient or reliable than a dozen other young corporals, all of whom, *Inshallah*, would one day make good steady platoon sergeants, and there were others coming on. It seems a trifling incident, but the C.O. who does not pray for good platoon sergeants does not exist.

It was at about this time that Major-General Ahmed Sudqi Pasha el Jundi, the second-in-command of the Legion, was retired. I was sorry, for he had always been polite and friendly to me.

Soon after Christmas, on 29th December to be exact, there was a conference at Brigade Headquarters, and Turki Hussein, the Brigade Major, gave a talk on the recent troubles. He explained the points in favour of the Baghdad Pact, so that commanding officers would be in a position to indoctrinate their soldiers. He pointed out that it did not mean that the Arab Legion would have to fight outside Jordan — a criticism that had been much in the minds of the anti-pact propagandists — that it had no adverse effect on the Arab League Defence Pact, or the Palestine Problem. There was not, as some had said, a secret agreement between the Turks and the Israelis.

He went on to say that in the event of future rioting firm action would be taken. Ring-leaders would be arrested and, if necessary, as many as six hundred of them would be sent to the prison camps in the desert. Gas bombs were to be issued to the troops, and curfews enforced in riotous towns.

The riots had been well organized with the object of undermining the country, and putting in a Government which would be a puppet of Egypt. In such a case the British would go, there would be an end of the subsidy, and the Jews could walk in when they felt like it.

This was fighting talk, but the mob had seen the weakness of the Government and had acquired a taste for power.

The lull was to last precisely twenty days.

CHAPTER VIII: ALARUMS AND EXCURSIONS

Early in January a company of 6 Regiment relieved us in the front line, and we moved into camp at Jiftlik where we formed a central reserve for the Arab Legion. From there we could be moved to any of the likely trouble spots. By 4th January the move was complete.

I formed Support Company into a temporary rifle company, leaving behind the older men to look after the heavy weapons. Said Saleh, since he knew the area well, was left in charge at Silat ed Dahr, while Salim Bakhet took command of the detachment at Ain Fara, where we left the 17-pounders. The Brigadier had arranged that if anything happened Salameh Etayek should return and act as second-in-command.

I was woken at four in the morning of 8th January and opened the front door to find a Naqib of the Divisional Signals, who handed me this message:

DT0071150

From: HQ 1 Div
To: 2 Bde — 9 Regt
TOP SECRET (.) 9 Regt will concentrate in the area near SALT where the JISR DAMIYA and JERICHO roads meet by 1000 hrs tomorrow 8 Jan 56

B. E. Luard Qaid.

Col. Young must be told immediately.

B.E.L.

I left Rafidia soon after with Juma'a driving, accompanied by Ahmed Qasim, the interpreter, and Abdulla Heikal and Hamed

Inad as orderlies. Omer, my batman, was to follow later in a truck which was to fetch him and my kit. We reached the officers' lines at Jiftlik before 0630, and found the camp beginning to stir.

I looked around for Khdayer, who shortly emerged from his tent muffled up in his greatcoat. I told him to leave the camp standing and move off as soon as the men had breakfasted. I had no information for him, though I supposed that trouble was expected in Amman; and I had no idea how long we would be away, not that it mattered much, for the bedouin take these moves in their stride — hardly strange considering their nomadic background. I left them to it.

We crossed Damiya Bridge and took the Arda road up the forbidding, precipitous range which lies to the East of the Jordan. We had not gone far when we met a squadron of the 2nd Armoured Car Regiment winding down on their way to reinforce Brigadier Green at Nablus. I stopped their commander and warned him that he would soon meet 9 Regiment on their way up, and that we did not want any collisions. These wise words were hardly out of my mouth, when turning a corner we came upon an armoured car on its side in the ditch. From its tracks one could see that the driver had gone near the edge of the precipice, and swinging over to his left at too high a speed, had turned over. The two members of the crew were groaning miserably in the back of a Land-Rover, while the driver was huddled in the ditch. Juma'a looked at him and told me there was nothing much the matter with him, but that he was shamming to avoid being asked awkward questions. A cold North wind was blowing, so I told the soldiers to move the casualties round the corner into cover, and wait for our Doctor to catch up. Mashour Mutlaq, one of my dispatch-riders, went to tell Urfan Johari what had happened. As usual on these occasions, there were flocks of jundis around the wreck, taking an unintelligent interest in the proceedings. Naturally their chief concern was to get the victims to hospital regardless of whether the journey killed them.

By 0945 the Regiment was assembled at its rendezvous. We closed the trucks up on the right of the road, and let the soldiers dismount. When the company commanders were assembled for a few minutes' talk, I found that Musayeb was sick and Muhamad Moazi was therefore commanding No. 1 Company. Leaving Abu Mudhish in charge, for Salameh had not yet appeared, I drove into Amman to find out what the form was. We arrived without incident, except that there were rocks across the road near Sweilleh. I knew that a few days earlier Qiada had moved to its new premises to the West of the City, for though the plumbing was not yet complete, tactical considerations came first. I found Jim Hutton's office and reported to him. I was to come under Brigadier Parry, whose Brigade Headquarters was at the Citadel, but he was not to launch the Regiment without first asking Qiada. Meanwhile rioters were stoning the Police Station at Salt, and I was to send a company to reinforce the police. Feisal Mite'b took my orders back to Abu Mudhish.

Brigadier Hutton told me that there had been rioting in Amman on the previous day and that the City was now under curfew. 3 Brigade were there in force, and the streets were empty of civilians as we drove up to the Citadel. At intervals there were small patrols of soldiers and every corner was guarded. Just beyond the Prime Minister's office there were signs of yesterday's rioting, where some Government office had been attacked; the street outside was strewn with burnt papers. Here and there were burnt-out cars. Brigadier Parry was away when I arrived, but he soon returned and told me that he had insufficient men to enforce the curfew in the streets East of the Palace; streets running along the main road that leads out to the Railway Station. He wanted me to arrest about forty men in that area as an example. I sent for a company to carry out this operation, and went back along the Salt road to meet them. Nazzal Hleyil appeared with 2 Company, going so fast that I could hardly stop them! It only took a minute or two to tell him and his platoon commanders what was going on. One platoon was to form a cordon at a bridge at the South end of the area, while two other platoons were to drive on as if going to Zerqa. On reaching the North end of the district to be searched they were to dismount quickly, fan out and beat back towards the cordon. We drove down into the town and along Feisal Street, passing a strong picket outside the Ottoman Bank. It was strange not to see a single vehicle, car, bus or taxi in this place where normally there is hardly room to park. We halted in a side street that leads to the Palace, and one platoon dismounted. Nazzal checked up that his men knew what to do, and when they were ready we drove slowly out on to the main road again and turned North. The cordon platoon gave us a couple of minutes and, leaving a few men to guard their 3-tonner, ran out on to the bridge. At the other end of the area, the rest of the company leaped from their vehicles, fixed bayonets and started their drive.

Curfew is intended as a punishment. In this quarter it was merely a holiday. Outside the cafes knots of men sat on little stools sunning themselves, for the cold morning wind had gone and it was now a perfect spring day. In garage yards and in every side street people gossiped and idled, vanishing like rabbits when the bedouin appeared, only to pop out again when they had passed. Every now and again someone would venture on a dash to the local grocer's shop. It was not long before we had twenty or thirty prisoners, the results of our first sweep. They were put in a 3-tonner and sent to the cage at Abdalli.

It was comparatively easy to clear the main street, although the pickets along it, men from some haderi gunner regiment, had long since lost all interest in the job, but the side-streets were another matter. Built on the almost precipitous hill-side, with flights of narrow steps running down between the houses, there was plenty of cover for anyone who felt he would like a little fresh air. Shouting "To your house! To your house! Don't go outside" knots of bedouin prowled around with rifle and bayonet, or with stout sticks and drove the people indoors. I went back to Headquarters, reported to the Brigadier and then returned to the Regiment.

SALT

Khdayer met me with the news that there had been shooting in Salt, when No. 1 Company on its way to relieve the police had been received with rocks, stones and firearms. Salameh had arrived and had taken No. 4 Company to reinforce the troops already there.

Second Lieutenant Muhamad Moazi with more valour than discretion had driven down the road to Salt in his Land-Rover followed by his whole company, including, quite unnecessarily the two 1-ton trucks containing his stores and reserve ammunition. When he neared the town many of the inhabitants were sitting on the hospital hill stoning the Police Station, which lay below them on the side of the hill, and had succeeded in smashing most of the windows and a sky-light in the roof. Muhamad Moazi drove straight past and never stopped until he came to the sharp turning where the road bends round to go on towards Jericho. Corporal Farhan Salman with No. 1 Platoon in a 3-tonner followed him. A large mob confronted them, and a fight ensued, in which one of the mob hit Farhan in the chin with a pistol, and was shot for his pains. An Iraqi recruit, Saoud Abdulla, ran forward and rescued the corporal, who had fallen to the ground. The two trucks arrived and these the Saltis proceeded to set on fire, removing them later into the town.

Meanwhile Rfeilan Awwad the colour-sergeant in command of 2 Platoon, had driven straight up the side road into the Police Station. He had listened to Muhamad Omer's orders, and interpreted them correctly. When he arrived he found a dozen policemen cowering inside the building while the Saltis showered rocks down on them. The first thing to be done was to clear the hill. Rfeilan deployed his platoon and led them up the slope in extended order, while the bearded corporal, Muhamad Wuhayid, wanted for murder in three countries, who was acting platoon sergeant, whipped in. The men of Salt are a mulish race, and greeted this charge with volleys of stones; from the edge of the town a few of the inhabitants joined in with rifles. Rfeilan marked the houses from which the firing came.

Meanwhile Cadet Addad Msayeh dismounted 3 Platoon and attacked the hospital hill from the East. The Saltis retired into the town leaving eleven casualties including seven dead or mortally wounded but taking with them two rifles and two boxes of ammunition, which they had stolen from the 1-tonners. When Addad advanced a gang of Saltis attacked his 3-tonner. The driver, a Belgawi bedouin from near Amman, called Flayeh Awwad, was hit by a stone, and fired hitting the man who had struck him. Some of the mob set fire to the canopy of the vehicle, but he managed to drive it away and put out the fire.

At the time I was exceedingly angry with Muhamad Moazi, and wished that Musayeb had been there to command his company. In fact it was just as well that Musayeb was absent since, as afterwards appeared, he had his doubts as to which side was going to come out on top, and kept out of the way! Muhamad admitted afterwards that he would have done better to take a look round before he drove straight into the hornets' nest, but in his favour it must be said that he used the minimum of force. He ceased fire long before the rioters dispersed because as he said, they were too good a target.

Khdayer clearly could not know the full facts so I drove down to see Salameh at the Police Station. The yard was littered with stones, but the Saltis were no longer to be seen. The landing outside the commandant's office was a litter of broken glass, splintered wood, rocks and dust. I found the District Commander, a little lieutenant-colonel, sitting at his desk, smoking. He was perfectly calm, and greeted me with the accustomed Arabic courtesy. His second-in-command had not his sang-froid. Coffee was served. After a while the notables arrived, summoned by the District Commander, and were ordered to produce the missing arms and vehicles. They were full of assurances that they would do their best, but clearly had not the least intention of living up to them. I spoke to Brigadier Hutton on the telephone, told him how things were, and requested permission to move into Salt and impose a curfew. However, there had been further outbreaks elsewhere and instead I was ordered to leave one platoon in Salt, move the Regiment to the outskirts of Amman and report to Qiada for further orders. Never a dull moment.

A platoon of 4 Company, under Mteir Dhahi, a strict and reliable officer, was left to garrison the hospital, for if that was held the Police Station was in no real danger. I told the Mukhtars that I would seek permission to search the town, and leaving Salameh to bring on the Regiment, I left for Amman.

When I reached Qiada late in the afternoon, I went at once to Jim Hutton's office where General Cooke and Colonel Luard had also set up their Headquarters. They told me that there had been serious rioting in Zerqa and that Colonel Lloyd had been killed. I was to take the Regiment to Zerqa and impose a curfew on the town. Salt could wait. In addition there were a number of political prisoners, communists and the like, to be moved under a strong guard from the Arab Legion camp near Amman Railway Station, to Mafraq. I decided to take the main body to Zerqa and to let Salameh escort the prisoners. A minor complication was that there had been some kind of a brawl in Ruseifa village, where two companies of 2 Regiment, on their way to reinforce the garrison of Zerqa, had been attacked. No details were available.

It was dark before the Regiment arrived. Salameh was summoned to Hutton's office, where I briefed him. Something in his manner aroused the Brigadier's suspicions and he asked me whether he could be relied upon.

"Oh, Salameh's all right," I replied.

The company and platoon commanders had been assembled meanwhile, and were waiting for me on the verandah of the guard-room, among them was Farhan Salman, his face bandaged, but unwilling to be sent to hospital. I explained what had happened in Zerqa and gave out my orders. Support Company, all picked men, would lead, and the column would halt on the hill overlooking Ruseifa, advancing from that point on foot. They had five minutes to talk to their men, and then we moved down through Amman to the Mohatta. Leaving the Regiment halted on the road I drove up to the gaol, where Salameh was seeing the prisoners into the vehicles. Warders and soldiers were milling about in the dark, and the prisoners were singing some song, which though I could not understand much of it, was evidently political and certainly unmusical. Perhaps they were merely trying to bolster up their morale, but they sounded positively triumphant. I told Salameh to make them keep quiet.

"Let them sing," he said, "they are not doing any harm."

"They can do as I say."

Although it was too dark to see his face, his voice and manner told me that he was unhappy. The Brigadier had been right in suspecting that he did not relish this task. It was almost as if he was afraid of these men; perhaps he was. Perhaps he thought they were going to come out on top, and maybe they thought so to. No doubt he thought I was a B.F., but then he had probably thought so for the last three years, and in the meanwhile I reckoned it would be time for the prisoners to start singing when they left our care. The concert ended, and I went on my way wishing that my highly trained second-in-command had remained in Divisional Headquarters, leaving me some less complicated assistant.

We reached Ruseifa without incident. Juma'a pulled in to the side, and I went back to the Adjutant's Land-Rover, which was following.

"All out! Dismount!"

The leading platoon went clattering past in the dark.

"Fix bayonets."

The platoon commander fanned his men out on both sides of the road, and started off down the hill. It was the Mortar

Platoon; Mifleh Salim, who was commanding, had risen to the rank of sergeant in five years — most unusual. Mseifer Murki joined us and we followed the soldiers exhorting them to keep their dressing properly. We swept down to the Police Station without seeing a soul or any sign of trouble; the inhabitants having had their fun had gone home. When we reached the bridge we came upon a crude road-block. The soldiers started flinging the rocks off the road, and down into the wadi, and after a few minutes there was room to pass. We re-mounted and pushed on towards Zerqa.

ZERQA

In a few minutes we reached the avenue of cypress trees which leads down to the Zerqa bridge, to be met by a scout car from the 1st Armoured Car Regiment, sent by Ray Leakey to guide us. The officer told me that there was a road-block in the main street. From the Police Post at the bridge I rang up Qiada and talked to Desmond Emms the G2, telling him that we had arrived, that all was quiet in Ruseifa, and that Salameh was by-passing Zerqa to the East.

We drove across the bridge and as we wound up the hill through the outskirts of Zerqa town it was beginning to rain. At the top of the hill where there are houses on both sides of the street, we found a double road block two or three feet high, made of large squared stones such as are used in building. No wheeled vehicle could pass. Instantly the Mortar Platoon began to hurl the obstacle aside. A few people appeared, whether hostile or merely passing we neither knew nor cared.

"To your houses!" They departed, hastened on their way by a volley of rocks.

A few minutes' work cleared the obstruction sufficiently to let the vehicles pass: I ordered Mifleh Salim to continue the advance, and we pushed on down the main street. On the right was a burnt-out Land-Rover — Lloyd's — but otherwise everything was normal. The rioters had all gone home when it got dark and we met nobody until, after passing between the Cinema Nasser and the Police Station, we came upon the detachment of 2 Regiment, drawn up to bar the way into Zerqa Camp. There may have been other troops as well, for a solid mass of soldiers, seemingly several hundred strong, blocked the road.

Not wishing them to open fire on us I ordered the men to halt and shouted: "Kateba Tis'a! 9 Regiment!"

"Ahlan wa Sahlan" (Welcome). We were greeted with enthusiasm — it was like an absurd parody of the relief of Lucknow. Ray Leakey emerged from somewhere and we walked on into the camp together. I told the officers that the streets were now empty.

Brigadier Lupton, the commander of the Arab Legion Artillery, was the senior officer present in Zerqa, and he had set up a headquarters in a building next to the telephone exchange, and opposite the main parade-ground. Here we found him with his Brigade Major, Mike Hunt; Dennis Freeman now commanding 4th Light A.A. Regiment and a number of other officers, British and Arab. He described the events of the day, and Mike produced something to keep the cold out.

It seems that during the morning there had been an attack on Zerqa Bridge, which was successfully defended by a young bedouin cadet with a troop of armoured cars. The attackers had got near enough to throw two 36 grenades at the soldiers — a most unusual deed, for in Jordan, unlike Cyprus, the usual weapons are stones and, occasionally, firearms but seldom bombs.

After a time a big mob gathered in the main street. First the schoolgirls, whose headmistress had thoughtfully provided them with a banner, then the schoolboys and the refugee basket boys who run errands in the town. Other refugees swelled the number, until in the end all Zerqa was out. There were even a few soldiers in civilian clothes; present perhaps from curiosity.

By this time the shops were shut. The police were unable to control the crowd, who were blocking the main Mafraq-Amman road with stones. After a time the Qaimakam, or Civil Governor, a man in his early thirties, went out and spoke to the crowd urging them to disperse. In vain.

The Brigadier decided to send troops to restore order. Lt.-Col. Lloyd and a company about ninety strong, formed for the occasion from the headquarters of 4 L.A.A., a haderi regiment, went out. It was very difficult to piece together the story of what happened because Patrick Lloyd was the only British officer present. It seems that they had reached the point from which we afterwards cleared the road-block and that the men were halted across the street, while the crowd retired into the alleyways. Patrick had left his Land-Rover and was some twenty or thirty yards from his men when he was knocked down by stones. The mob rushed out into the street and milled around him; one of them shot him in the head with a small automatic pistol, about .25 calibre. His Land-Rover was burnt and some tear-gas bombs stolen. The soldiers did not fire. After a time two soldiers went forward, took up Lloyd's body, and carried him into a nearby clinic. Brigadier Lupton, Leakey, Hunt and others went out with part of 2 Regiment, which had arrived from Amman, and brought Lloyd back, but he was dead before he reached the camp.

Pat Lloyd had commanded 4 L.A.A. Regiment for about a year, and his death was a great shock to his men and to us all. It is easy to condemn his soldiers for not opening fire in his defence, and I feel that bedouin soldiers would have used their rifles. For the haderi soldiers the strain was becoming too great. The mob were their kith and kin, and at least to that extent the soldiers sympathised with the rioters.

I put No. 1 Company into Zerqa Police Station, and the rest of the Regiment went to the Armoured Car lines. The curfew was to begin at daybreak. David Smith, whose house was only a hundred yards from the Command Post, invited me to stay with him.

About four o'clock in the morning I got up and went down to the Police Station. It was clear that although the schoolchildren went over the top first, the main "enemy" were the refugees, who inhabit a well-defined camp, lying immediately East of the railway, and only about a hundred yards South of the wire which surrounds Zerqa Camp. The cantonment itself was not my responsibility, but was defended by an ad hoc force commanded by Lt.-Col. John Close, of the Arab Legion Driving School. It seemed to me that if the refugees could be kept from getting into the town and joining the other inhabitants the battle would be half won.

To understand what is going on in Jordan today it is absolutely necessary to know something of the refugee question. The problem dates from 1948, when four-fifths of the Arab inhabitants of what is now Israel were driven from their homes. Half a million of these people now live in Jordan, some on the East Bank and some on the West, mostly in squalid camps administered by U.N.R.W.A. Few have any work, for they have been persuaded by politicians that if they lose their status as refugees they will lose their right to compensation, and U.N.R.W.A. schemes to resettle them or provide employment on a large scale are regarded with deep suspicion. The refugees fear that such schemes will not succeed, and will merely result in the loss of their ration cards.

The majority of the refugees, who make up something like one-third of the total population of Jordan, were fellahin, though some were nomadic tribesmen of the Beersheba bedouin. The fellahin were peasant proprietors, tilling land which had been in their families for centuries. Abu Yusef, my neighbour in Rafidia, who refused to lose his individualism in a camp, formerly owned a farm near Jaffa with five hundred orange trees. Then he had his own house with two or three rooms and was, by local standards, well-to-do. Now he lives in a hovel and makes a precarious living by casual labour.

Many of the refugee camps are in the Jordan valley. There are roughly seventy thousand in the three camps at Jericho, and perhaps another ten thousand at Karameh. There are camps near Jenin and Tulkarm, and two big ones at Nablus. But from the internal security point of view the worst problem is that every big town has its refugee population. The traditional costumes of Palestine are common in the streets of Amman; Zerqa has fully ten thousand refugees, mostly slum-dwellers. Even little places like Ajlun have their quota.

An Arab boy of fourteen, whose world crashed about him in 1948, is now twenty-one, and so a bitter and revengeful generation has grown up in exile, and what we have seen so far is nothing to what may lie ahead if the Palestine problem is not settled. The refugees hate the Jews, but they also hate those Western nations whom they blame for permitting the Israelis to carve a state out of Palestine. Most of these people have nothing to do except sit about gossiping. The agitator, whether he is paid by the Egyptians or the Communists, has, therefore, no lack of raw material. A few impassioned words about their wrongs, a few anti-British slogans, a banner or two, and a basketful of stones are all the ingredients needed to start a first-class riot.

In 1953 Miss W. A. Coate, a good friend of the refugees who for the past five years had been in charge of a relief centre in Zerqa nevertheless wrote of them: "We have constantly on our doorstep all the riff-raff of the Jaffa port: touts, pickpockets, prostitutes and many unemployables." Jaffa, the scene of the riots in 1921, the first serious disturbances between Arab and Jew during the Mandate, like most ports had its fair share of roughs. All too many of these had come to Zerqa where, with the local school-children, they formed the rank and file of the Zerqa riots. It was clear to me that the refugee camp was going to be my chief problem.

I deployed No. 4 Company under Hammad Faleh along the railway line, facing East, but with a few men behind them to picket the road junctions on the main street. The embankments and cuttings would give 4 Company a little cover should there be any shooting.

The roof of the Police Station was a fairly good observation post, and I had a telephone extension put there. A section of riflemen manned the parapet. When it got light a police officer went round with a public-address equipment mounted in a one-ton truck, announcing that there was to be a curfew, and that anyone who emerged was liable to be shot. Patrols scoured the streets of the town.

There were various complications. In the first place numbers of civilians, ranging from mechanics to sweepers and including many of the domestic servants of British officers, work in Zerqa camp. All these emerged with innocent looks on their faces, and started in the direction of the cantonment. Another contingent came dribbling down to the Police Station to meet the trucks which daily take them to work at the British Ordnance Depots. With all these people coming and going on their more or less legitimate occasions it was small wonder that the other inhabitants also began to emerge. The sun came out and so did the refugees.

Although the remainder of the town was by now reasonably quiet, from my vantage point I could see numbers of people moving about in the refugee camp. At the main entrance a large group of idlers was standing; at almost every corner there were knots of people, who were paying no attention whatever to the warnings given by the public-address equipment. I turned to Faleh Soud, the sniper, who stood at my side, and ordered him to put a bullet over the heads of one of these groups. He fired and they vanished. Pointing out yet another party I ordered him to fire again, and once more the curfew-breakers scattered, but the big group remained unmoved. I therefore sent word to 4 Company to advance and break them up. This was done, but the people merely scattered into the lanes and alleys. There was still a great deal of movement. I left the roof of the Police Station and walked across to see Hammad Faleh, who had succeeded by now in driving the people well away from the railway line. Looking up the lanes of the camp one could see men sunning themselves in their doorways, and women fetching water. This curfew was no punishment. I reorganized 4 Company's dispositions, detailing a pair of men to watch each lane, and assembled the remainder to act as patrols to sally forth and arrest any men who, after further warning, remained outdoors. The people were quick off their marks and as soon as we made a move they vanished. However, by sending the patrols up lanes parallel to those where they were standing about, we soon collected a sizeable bag. Those arrested were sent under escort to the Police Station and handed over.

At the West end of the camp we were beginning to get the upper hand, though down at the East end one could still see people moving about much as they pleased. It was at this juncture that I saw one of the police infantry walking into the camp along with two young men who had been arrested by my orders not twenty minutes earlier. Instantly a patrol dashed out and intercepted them before they could disappear among the houses. They were brought back.

"Where are you going? I sent these men to prison."

"They were released by the Qaimakam, sir."

"Return to the Qaimakam and tell him that if he wishes to release the people I arrest he should tell me first." I do not know whether he delivered my message, but I imagine that he told the Civil Governor that I was incensed.

I returned to the Police Station, and meeting the Qaimakam outside, walked up and down with him talking. He was slightly apologetic about the released prisoners.

"Those two young men you arrested again, they are quite all right. Their father is my friend."

"Nevertheless they were breaking the curfew."

"Won't you release them? They won't do it again."

"I don't imagine they will. I have sent them to the Brigadier."

Changing his tack he told me that he was quite satisfied with the way the people were obeying the curfew. I said that I was not. He smiled and tried to persuade me that all was well enough, making it clear that he disapproved of my showing my nose outside the Police Station. Maybe he feared that I would come to a bad end; or maybe he wished to shield the people of Zerqa from the consequences of their misdeeds. Although I disagreed with him on practically every point, he was in fact a charming and pleasant person. It was his ambition to run with the hare and hunt with the hounds. If the people of Zerqa were going to be punished it was not going to be by him. He thoroughly disapproved of murder and mob violence, but he also admired Colonel Nasser and condemned the Baghdad Pact, and frankly told me so. For him, and for the gunners of the 4th Artillery Regiment the strain was just too great, for the rioters were their own kith and kin, struggling for something they themselves approved.

In this storm the bedouin were our sheet-anchor. But it looked as if the strain was telling even on them, for during the night three Syrians from No. 1 Company had deserted, taking their rifles. Perhaps they had been alarmed by the skirmish in Salt, perhaps they were afraid of becoming involved in a blood feud. By an unlucky chance I had been in Amman during the action at Salt, and, not being an eyewitness, could not really tell what had upset these men. In so far as Zerqa was concerned I intended to keep my eye on the men and to determine the state of their morale for myself. I could see no other way of being sure who was to be depended upon and who was not. After a reasonably amicable conversation, in which we agreed to differ, I left the Qaimakam and went back towards the railway line. Abu Mudhish, who also wanted me to return to the Police Station, came up. In Salameh's absence he was the senior Arab officer, and he knew that, if somebody put a bullet into me, he would find himself in charge, a thought which appalled him. I told him he had no cause for alarm, and sent him to take charge of Regimental Headquarters.

The Qaimakam clearly had not the least intention of enforcing the curfew. Abu Mudhish, an amiable easy-going officer, who lived in Zerqa, and was no thunderbolt at the best of times, was obviously out of his depth. The ball was in my court.

The time had come to clamp down on the East end of the refugee camp. I had noticed that Cadet Hussein Warid could be relied upon to obey orders, and while some of the men were priming gas-bombs I told him to pick the best soldiers from his platoon to come with us. Ahmed Qasim had remained in the Police Station, but Juma'a, Abdulla Heikal, Hamed Inad and Omer, my batman, were all with the party, perhaps twenty in all, which soon afterwards advanced to clear the rest of the refugee camp. It was up to Hammad Faleh and the remainder of 4 Company to ensure that the streets stayed clear after we had passed, for until Salameh should return from Mafraq we had insufficient men to picket the whole camp. After the doings of the previous day I did not wish to ask the Brigadier for gunners, nor could I spare any troops from the rest of the town.

We cleared the Northern street of the camp without much trouble, making the people shut their yard doors and close their shutters. The police van still patrolled round warning the people to keep indoors. Moving through the side alleys we would emerge into a lane to see numbers of people wandering about and amusing themselves as if nothing was happening. Sometimes we fired a few shots into a wall near them, sometimes we lobbed tear-gas bombs among them, and by appearing where we were least expected, despite our inadequate numbers, we gradually got the place quiet.

There were two main difficulties. One was that the lavatories and water taps were in the middle of the street. The women kept coming out of their houses to fetch water, and it was very difficult to prevent this, for the soldiers, being good Moslems, were extremely embarrassed at having to talk to other men's wives. The other difficulty, as we quickly discovered, was that a great number of soldiers, mostly from base units, had married refugee girls and were living in the camp, or were refugees who had managed to get themselves enlisted. These people much resented being made to conform to the curfew. Once coming unawares upon a bunch of young roughs, loitering defiant in a lane, we charged and routed them. Hotly pursued by the bedouin they stamped down a narrow alley, only wide enough for one abreast. The leading refugee was no athlete and blocked the path so that I was able to overtake the last man, who kept looking over his shoulder and cannoning into the man ahead of him. I was armed with a swordstick, which though blunt glinted fiercely in the sunlight and lent him wings. Another time we broke up a party with a couple of gas bombs, which we threw without due regard for the wind. As we were not wearing gasmasks, for a few minutes we stood in one of the by-ways weeping like children. Abdulla Heikal, who as a boy had fallen off his camel and broken his nose, did not stop crying for days. Eventually we were able to go round the whole refugee camp without seeing anybody out of doors.

We had given them a good fright, and nobody had been killed in the process. I decided to return to my headquarters and await developments. On the way back to the Police Station we ran into Salameh Bey, who had just returned from Mafraq, having completed his mission.

"This is like a battle," he said. "These people are our friends. They are not doing any harm."

"Not now, they are not," I agreed ungrammatically. "You should have seen them two hours ago."

During the course of the morning Brigadiers Lupton and Mitford and I were summoned to Qiada for a conference. I sent for Salameh and told him, not without misgivings, that he was in charge, and that it was up to him to enforce the curfew strictly. During 1955 he had built two houses, each with a shop, in Zerqa and was not going to risk his popularity in what had come to be his home town. He asked what the conference was about, and I said I did not know, adding "perhaps trouble is expected with the Jews and we are going back to Palestine". At this he brightened up.

Brigadier Lupton drove me into Amman in his Land-Rover. Neither of us had the least notion what the conference would be about, but our guess was that Qiada wanted to withdraw some of our troops, and we spent most of the journey trying to work out the minimum force needed for Zerqa. Our guess was quite wrong. The idea broached by Jim Hutton was that the whole of the Zerqa refugee camp should be cordoned and searched for arms, house by house. The refugees who had behaved so badly deserved this extra punishment. For this purpose we were to be given another battalion as cordon, and 9 Regiment was to do the search.

When I was asked for my opinion I said that I did not think it would work. Too many of the soldiers lived in Zerqa, nor could we rely on the support of either the Qaimakam or my second-in-command. In any case there were probably very few arms in the camp. So long as the curfew was strictly imposed that was punishment enough. This was also the opinion of the two Brigadiers.

As a result of this meeting it was agreed by Glubb Pasha that Salameh should return to his duties as D.A.Q.M.G. of the 1st Division, as soon as Saoud Rashdan could be brought back from England. Thus the conference ended satisfactorily and the special factors affecting Zerqa were appreciated; the most important being that so many officers and soldiers, both bedouin and haderi, had their families living in the town.

As we drove up the hill into Zerqa we saw the people walking about as if the curfew had been lifted. I found Salameh and a number of the officers sitting on the roof of the Police Station talking to Abdulla Qa'ad, whose squadron of armoured cars was under my command. I knew that this officer did not enjoy the Pasha's confidence but I did not know the reason. I attempted, without much success, to allay Salameh's curiosity as to what had occurred at the conference.

It did not take long to re-establish the curfew, for we now had the troops who had returned from Mafraq and were able to put a network of pickets and patrols all over the refugee camp. All I had to do now was to drive round the streets and ensure that my patrols were strict and efficient. There were lighter moments. Once turning a corner I saw a man lolling in his doorway, his arms folded, with a "can't catch me" look on his face. As we wheeled past him I pulled out my luger and put a bullet through the glass fanlight above his head. The shower of broken glass, plaster and splinters hardly had time to reach his head before he vanished like a rabbit into its hole. O'Kelly himself might have been proud of such a shot! And it made Juma'as day for him,; his sense of humour was always a little primitive.

On the 10th I was early at the Police Station. Brigadier Lupton had made arrangements with John Close to limit and control the numbers of civilian employees working in the cantonment, and there was therefore very much less illegal movement on this day. I sent Salameh to inspect our detachment at Salt, and attended to the curfew in Zerqa myself.

I spent much time touring around to the various companies and speaking to the soldiers to make sure that they understood the object of the operation, and to gauge their reaction to it.

They were extremely indignant that a C.O. had been murdered, and still more that his soldiers had done nothing about it. During the days that followed there were no more desertions, and when, a few days later, Saoud Rashdan returned to the fold I felt that everything was under control again. Saoud was a straightforward character, and it was not only I that welcomed his return. The reaction of my officers was interesting. "If you won't be a wolf, the wolves will eat you," was the comment of Abu Mudhish. Nazzal Hleyil's version of this proverb was: "If you are a grain the chicken will eat you." No man can serve two masters.

In order to let the populace buy bread, draw water, and so forth the curfew was lifted for an hour each afternoon. At first we had trouble getting them to go home again. They were an obstinate lot, and not unduly impressed by foot soldiers; the one thing that put the fear of God into them was cavalry. Traditionally the fellahin of Palestine and Transjordan lived in dread of the police cavalry: a sergeant in the gendarmerie being thought rather senior to a District Governor. The cavalry school was at Zerqa, and we had therefore the assistance of old Captain Rashid, G.C., who, with a dozen cavaliers, soon had the inhabitants on the move.

AJLUN

In Zerqa the curfew was continued for some days, and after three days' rehearsal the people were getting to know their part; if it was tedious for the soldiers it was ten times more so for them.

But if Zerqa was quiet there were troubles elsewhere. Ajlun, to everyone's surprise, now chimed in. The people came in from the surrounding villages and began to break up the hospital. Brigadier Lupton ordered me to send a company there, to work under the orders of the police; a section, at least, was to garrison the hospital. No. 4 Company had good officers and had done well in Zerqa, moreover; I was now allowed to recall Mteir Dhahi's platoon from Salt, and so it was Hammad Faleh that departed into the mountains of Gilead. He had served nearly twenty years in the Jeish, and had harried the rebel gangs through the steep valleys of the Ajlun district in the far-off days of 1939. He arrived without incident, but at about 11.30 on the 13th demonstrators advanced on the hospital: the garrison fired a few rounds, and dispersed them without damage or casualties, except that one of the rioters was made prisoner.

Saleh Daham, the M.T.O., returned to Zerqa bringing with him the American Doctor and his parents, who were taken to the American Embassy in Amman. The Doctor said that £10,000 would not repair the damage done; the pharmacy was wrecked, windows and doors broken. A neighbouring house was burned as well as the school, and a tent near the Castle, belonging to Point 4. The telephone lines had been cut between Ajlun and Irbid. Hammad Faleh's report reached Zerqa about midday. I was pleased to find that the old gentleman had taken it upon himself to impose a curfew.

At approximately 8 p.m. he had arrived at the hospital, where the Company was met by Rais Saleh Agrabawi, the Derak[16] commander there, who was in charge of the district, and explained the situation. Hussein Warid's platoon was left at the hospital, and the remainder of the company spent the night at Sub-District H.Q. Next morning the District Commander arrived with a list of the mukhtars, teachers and students suspected of causing the troubles, most of whom were arrested and sent to Irbid prison. On the third day Hammad proceeded

---

[16] Police cavalry.

to Anjara village, where he imposed curfew and collected suspected persons who were sent to Irbid. He stayed there two days. On the fifth day he moved on to Ibein and Ibelein villages, surrounded them, imposed curfew and arrested suspected persons. On the sixth day he withdrew on receiving a signal to say that a platoon from 4 Regiment was to relieve him.

In concluding his written report Hammad said: "I would like to inform you that we were very strict with the instigators of the trouble and the suspects." This I believe, for I heard afterwards that after rebuking a seditious school-teacher he chastised him with his walking-stick.

In making his report Hammad mentioned the good work of Waqil Warwir Hishal, whose ability and keenness had, it seems, impressed the officer commanding the mounted police at Ajlun, and recommended his promotion to Second Lieutenant! Warwir, of the Sirhan, who seemed a sullen, stupid sort of man, had left us in 1953, and after short periods in numerous regiments reappeared in 1955, via the National Guard. Eventually a letter came from Qiada saying that he was to be discharged. I heaved a sigh of relief, but at once the more senior officers were upon me. "He has many children and wives." "He has eighteen years' service." "*Wellahi*, he is wronged," and nothing would serve, but that this doom must be reversed. The Pasha intervened and all was well. Presumably Warwir was always a good man at heart; be that as it may, from this day forth he never failed to give satisfaction.

On the 13th the cavalry, who had been so useful on the previous days, were taken away, as they were going to ride through Ajlun district to show the flag, and eat the chickens. I had 4 Company away at Ajlun and by day two platoons of

Support Company were at Ruseifa, keeping open the Amman — Zerqa road.

To replace these I was given a composite company of gunners under an officer named Kemal, who had one of the finest moustaches in the Arab Legion. Brigadier Lupton was anxious that the gunners should take a part in the proceedings, as he felt that their morale had suffered because of events on the 8th, and so it was arranged that from 4.30 p.m. they would patrol with No. 2 Company. Patrols, each of not less than four men, were to be composed of equal numbers from 9 Regiment and 4 L.A.A. Regiment. Nazzal Hleyil, commanding No. 2 Company had his H.Q. at the boys' school near the Old Tower, and was in wireless communication with the Command Post in Zerqa Camp. I signed my orders at 1 p.m. and shortly afterwards Kemal and Nazzal arrived to tie up the details.

At 4.30 the gunners marched out of Zerqa Camp, wearing their steel helmets and with their rifles at the trail. I watched them from the roof of the Police Station, and they looked as if they meant business. Why had these men put up such a miserable performance on the 8th? Perhaps they had not been trained for the job, or perhaps it was asking too much to expect them to fire on a mob of their own countrymen. I felt confident that they would be all right with Nazzal, who was nothing if not solid and steady.

Since the cavalry had left I expected trouble getting the people home after the break in the curfew that afternoon, but by this time we had them well drilled and they all went home on time. They were fed up, and the public-address van went round making it quite clear that we were willing to keep the curfew going as long as they showed any ill discipline.

For the rest of our time at Zerqa I was able to pay a little attention to the turnout and administration of the Regiment, which, as always during operations, had begun to fall off. I used to parade the Regiment each morning on the square in Zerqa Camp, and after inspecting the men, practise them in various drills, which might be useful when our duties involved aid to the civil power.

In Nablus, as I heard, things were quiet, but Brigadier Green had sent his wife and mine away to stay with the Galletlys near Jerusalem. Joan joined me at Zerqa a few days later. Salim Bakhet's force had been attacked by the refugees of Ain Fara and had been forced to shoot one in self defence.

These were strange days in Jordan. In Ramthe the people had rebelled and moved the posts demarcating the frontier line between Syria and Jordan. The Syrian flag flew over their town! To add injury to insult they stoned the Minister of Defence. That was a mistake. A Special Force, largely composed of bedouin, was sent under Ali Hiyari to suppress them, which he did in no uncertain manner. A hundred rifles were demanded and a very considerable fine was exacted. Every house was made to fly the flag of Jordan.

I now heard from General Cooke that we also were to form part of a similar force under Qaimakam Sadiq Shara'.

CHAPTER IX: SPECIAL FORCE THREE

The Regiment remained in Zerqa for about a week, but on the 22nd before dark we concentrated near Shunet Nimrin, South of the Amman-Jericho road, in the stony plain between the hills and the Dead Sea.

Besides the Regiment I had a squadron from the 1st Armoured Car Regiment and two companies of 40 National Guard Regiment under Captain Fareed el Kutub. There was also a small detachment of engineers with mine-detectors, and a public-address unit. Police, infantry and cavalry, were to join us at Ain-es-Sultan next day. I called together the company commanders and briefed them. When I had done I sent my Adjutant, Khdayer Qa'aid, with a few men to Allenby Bridge to ensure that nobody should slip across and give the alarm.

At one o'clock in the morning we drove off. I was leading and controlling the move by wireless. When we reached the Eastern outskirts I halted the vehicles, debussed and advanced on foot. No. 1 Company, under Abu Mudhish, who was responsible for the cordon on the South side, was leading. Khalaf Ghassib with 3 Company took the West, and Hammad Faleh with 4 Company the North. Support Company under Mseifa Murki was to prowl about inside the camp and keep the people indoors; Nazzal Hleyil with 2 Company had gone to the big Police Station at Jericho to act as force reserve. The East side of the camp, which was very open, was cordoned by the armoured-car squadron with the two companies of National Guards under command.

By 0500 hours the camp had been surrounded. Nobody was astir, it was cold and rather misty and everything was as quiet as the grave. At five o'clock I told Muhamad Awwad el Harbi to start touring around, and announcing that there was a curfew and nobody was to stir abroad. His voice, sounding strangely deep in the still air, began to boom out over the public-address equipment.

As soon as the curfew was well under way Saoud Rashdan and his search parties started operations. Patrols of picked men, under Sukheil Hammad, Hussein Warid and Abdulla Salim el Harbi, each accompanied by a policeman, visited every house, confiscating arms and arresting their owners. It was not long before the first prisoner reached my headquarters. Mahmoud Hamdan Hussein had been found in possession of a sten, a magazine and seven rounds, which he alleged he had owned since 1948. This was not unlikely, for the magazine was so rusty that it no longer fitted the gun. Mahmoud was a pleasant young man, who managed to appear very innocent.

The next prize was a subversive letter, which with a dagger and an old revolver was found in the house of Khaled Abdel Hadi, who was away. Brahim Mahmoud had a pistol and three rounds besides a dagger, but the next two captives, Fawzi Hussein Mahmoud and Ahmed Muhamed Abdel Hadi, only had daggers, which are so commonly worn by the Palestinians as to be unworthy of notice. And so it went on. Shakir Muhamad Abdulla was found to possess a pamphlet of the Tahreer party, but he himself was not there. Two old rifles, a bayonet and another pistol completed the collection. Those who only had daggers were soon released and departed thankfully.

The search was not completed that day and on the next no more arms were found. It was not that the searchers flagged, but that the refugees found means to dispose of their weapons during the night. In any case they had nothing but antiques.

Tirrell's men at Akbat Jaba found a far more formidable armament.

At the same time a search for suspected ringleaders was in progress. A number of those on our list really lived in Nuweimeh camp, which was the responsibility of the Hashemite Regiment, but about a dozen were found in Ain-es-Sultan. Some, like Muhamad Ismail Shatir and Suleiman Moharib, were mere boys, the former about fifteen and the latter seventeen years of age. The younger Palestinian refugees have nothing to lose, and, oppressed by a feeling of insecurity, are always to the fore in riots and demonstrations, whether they know what they are about or not.

There were only two mukhtars in the camp, which made it rather difficult to deal with the people. The public-address system was invaluable for giving out general instructions, but the more subtle influence of trusted and known local leaders was lacking. One of the mukhtars was known to have been present in the attack on the Police Station, but his story was that he had been trying to stop the boys who were stoning the building. In cold blood, days after the event, it was impossible to arrive at the truth. The only thing was to give the people a good shock to discourage them from rioting in the future. One way of doing this was to arrest curfew-breakers, and detain them for a time at R.H.Q., where they were confined in one of the school-rooms. But there was far less curfew-breaking than at Zerqa, which is, of course, far larger, and where we did not have the use of Austers. The aircraft undoubtedly made the people feel uneasy, and flying overhead one could see them scuttling indoors as the plane approached. By wireless, Verey light or by swooping down one could indicate areas where people were moving about, and in a matter of seconds a patrol on foot or in a Land-Rover could pounce on the offenders.

The North-East part of the camp was mostly inhabited by Beersheba bedouin, who gave no trouble at all. One man of 4 Company found himself posted outside his parents' home, and was permitted to remain with them while we were there on condition that they at least should not break the curfew. The Beersheba bedouin had a number of camels which were normally taken outside the camp to graze. During the two hours each afternoon when the women were allowed to go to the spring, we permitted the boys to take the animals out to feed.

The camp, which is extremely dirty and poverty stricken is very badly built, many of the houses having no yards. A walled court is a usual feature of moslem houses, for there the women can sit unwatched. In time of curfew the people of Zerqa or Amman do not necessarily remain indoors, for most of them can sit unseen in their high-walled gardens. The people of Ain-es-Sultan merely sat on their doorsteps. The younger ones were chased inside or arrested, but there was not much one could do with a venerable patriarch — except take his photograph. After we reached the camp the first people astir were some of the old men assembling at the mosque for prayer. One did not feel disposed to interfere with them.

Touching the South end of the refugee camp stands the oldest city in the world, excavated in recent years by Miss Kenyon, who arrived to carry on with the digging while our operations were in progress. The great mound formed by this ancient city was too good a vantage point to be ignored, and I placed a section at the North end to watch one corner of the camp. Once on my rounds I went to visit these men, and found a bedu emerging from the depths of the great trench cut by the archaeologists. Perhaps he had been examining the wall which Joshua brought low; but more probably he had found a use for the trench for which it had not been intended.

The inhabitants of Ain-es-Sultan were simple folk, and so were some of their neighbours outside the camp on the Jericho side, who hearing the loud-hailer announce the curfew thought it applied to them as well and did not emerge until there was a break, when they came down to draw water with the rest. Listening to the talk of the women and young girls as they went down to the spring it was evident that they were much impressed by "the tanks," as they called our armoured cars. The well from which they draw their water, and which gives its name to the camp, is separated from ancient Jericho only by the road. This spring has perhaps been used by man for a longer period than any other in the world.

Not a shot was fired during our stay at Ain-es-Sultan. The force withdrew on the night 25th/26th January, handing over to two companies of the Hashemite Regiment and one of the National Guard.

Once more we concentrated at Shunet Nimrin.

KARAMEH

Karameh is a village of about twenty thousand refugees, including at least six thousand able-bodied men, who have been unemployed for eight years. Miss Coate describes the place aptly when she says it is "situated in a sandy, treeless waste, unendurably hot for much of the year. The people are of the lowest grade, ignorant, fanatical, and often violent".

Their most recent outburst had been a ferocious attack on the local police post, during which they had injured an officer and made off with two horses. "Naturally," writes Miss Coate, "among people living in such misery and insecurity political propagandists and agitators gain a ready hearing. No senior official of U.N.R.W.A. is permitted to enter the camp without police protection. Very few tourists or visitors are taken there. The degradation and demoralization of these forgotten people is almost unbelievable." These words were written in 1953, and it must not be imagined that conditions have improved much in the three years that have passed since they were penned. It is conceivable that if the Palestine problem were justly settled these people might become normal law-abiding citizens. Perhaps it is now too late and they are past hope.

These considerations were not uppermost in my mind on the night of 25th January. It was my affair to impose a curfew on these miserable people and to have their houses searched for arms. I had much the same force as before, except that 2 Company had returned and I had more armoured cars, and this time Ray Leakey was commanding them in person.

Before withdrawing from Ain-es-Sultan, and realizing that everybody, soldiers and refugees alike, would know that something was up, I gave out that the force was destined for Zerqa. It was a moonlit night, and so we were able to drive to within striking distance of Karameh with very few lights. By 5 a.m. all the troops were in position, and once again this was achieved without reconnaissance, although I was allowed to look at the place from the air beforehand. All the company commanders had air photographs on which their positions were marked for them. Karameh is ten miles north of Shunet Nimrin on the road east of and parallel with the Jordan. It is a fairly regular rectangle and stretches for nearly a mile on either side of the road. I put the armoured cars down the main street at the intersections of the laterals, and gave each rifle company a block of side-streets and buildings.

Once more Saoud Rashdan commanded the search but this time he had ten parties each under an officer or warrant officer. The people of Karameh, warned by what had been happening in the Jericho camps, had used their period of grace to get rid of their weapons, and we only found one Belgian pistol and a shotgun, both of which were properly licensed. This was no fault of Sadiq Shara's, for he had declared before the operations began that Special Force 3 was strong enough to take on Karameh and the Jericho camps at the same time. The only other arms found belonged to some bedouin enrolled by the Sherif Nasir, King Hussein's uncle, to safeguard his property in the district.

I set up my Headquarters in the school, and later in the day was joined by Sadiq, who personally interviewed the various mukhtars and a number of people who had been arrested. Nearly all the schoolmasters had been prominent during the disturbances and they were brought in for questioning, much to their disgust.

We had plenty of troops at Karameh and there was no difficulty in enforcing a strict curfew, though the people were hostile and sullen, quite unlike those of Ain-es-Sultan, who, though bewildered, had been rather friendly than otherwise. At Karameh the curfew and the search were carried out by the soldiers with gusto and efficiency, and the two companies of 40 National Guard Regiment under Rais Fareed el Ku tub were a valuable part of the force. The weather deteriorated during the operation, there was drizzle, and then a strong wind lashed the sand across the camp. This did nothing to improve tempers.

Sadiq Shara' was easy to work for. Always pleasant and confident, he left the regimental commanders to get on with the job, although he was always insisting that British C.O.s should not enter the camps themselves. Nobody has yet convinced me that you can command a regiment by remote control, and I did not propose to try.

One night Ray Leakey gave us dinner in his caravan, and afterwards we tackled Sadiq on a number of current problems. He is a graduate of the Staff College at Camberley, and he told us that although he had enjoyed himself in England, he had been very unfavourably impressed by the extent to which the country was governed and controlled by the Jews. We discussed the recent rioting, and he said:

"I have taken part in many demonstrations."

We were considerably surprised.

"Yes," he went on. "When I was a student in Irbid, before the last war we often had demonstrations, and I was one of the leaders. We used to march round the town for a couple of hours, and then at the end some of us would go to the Municipality and write down various points we wanted put right. Then we all went home. But there was no burning cars, no putting stones in the road. That is going too far, and it has got to be stopped."

We questioned him on his views regarding the rate of Arabization in the Jeish, and he assured us with confidence that Arab officers were already perfectly capable of commanding brigades. Perhaps rather tactlessly I pointed out that few indeed of the Arab officers had any experience of modern warfare.

On 28th January, Special Force 3 dispersed, and the Regiment returned to Jiftlik. The Hashemite Regiment went with Special Force 4 under Fawwaz Maher, which carried out punitive operations in the Hebron district.

One day soon after we returned to Jiftlik, Ahmed Qasim, my interpreter, blurted out: "I'm sorry I've been so useless in these last troubles, but you know, after all, I'm a bloody refugee myself!"

CHAPTER X: FINALE

We lingered at Jiftlik for some days although we were not again called out in aid of the civil power. I was anxious to get the Regiment back to normal soldiering, but we were still required as a reserve until the Hebron area had been settled. Salt got away scot-free but the lost vehicles were returned. One minor repercussion of the skirmish there was that certain Arab officers who lived there spread it about that, being incensed at the murder of Colonel Lloyd, I had launched my Regiment against Salt to take revenge. This was not the case. Quite apart from the fact that I was not personally engaged in the affair at Salt, but sent the company there by order of the Chief of Staff, I did not hear of the outrage in Zerqa until several hours after the fight at Salt. I cite this as typical of the wild rumours that fly about even among educated Arabs. Far more preposterous stories than this are believed, so long as they do not offend their prejudices.

If regular officers could persuade themselves of the truth of such tales it was scarcely surprising that other ranks of the National Guard should harbour similar ideas. On 30th January a bedouin corporal saw one of the National Guard hanging about for a long time near the entrance to our camp. The corporal went up to him and asked what he wanted, to which the man replied that he wished to speak to me personally on a matter of great importance. He was told that I was not present, but that the information could be passed on to me.

"Well, let us go far from here where I can tell you privately." He related how that morning he had gone to the camp of 42

National Guard Regiment to do his laundry. When he arrived he found two men of that regiment similarly occupied.

"Good morning, Brethren; may I wash my clothes here?" "Welcome. Are you from 40 Regiment?"

"I am."

"Where have you been all this time?"

"With 9 Regiment on special duty at Ain-es-Sultan and Karameh."

"Is it true that the Qaid killed many of the refugees there, as we hear?"

"I never heard this, and indeed our whole force never fired a round."

After this the men from 42 Regiment said to this soldier: "*Wellahi*, you are not faithful. Had we been there we would have shot this Qaid, for these people are Colonialists." One of them, speaking in an emotional way, said: "*Inshallah* the Pasha will visit our regiment and I will shoot him, and the Qaid if he is with him."

The National Guardsman from 40 Regiment returned to his camp, put away his clothes, and then went directly to 9 Regiment to tell me this story. The corporal reported this story to one of my officers, who came that evening to my house at Rafidia and told me. It was not difficult to identify the two disaffected soldiers whose names were Ameen Abdel Rahim of Jema'in and Hussein Said Atallah of Kufr Haris. The matter was reported to Brigade Headquarters. I heard afterwards that they were arrested and sent to prison in Nablus. They alleged that their words were not intended seriously, and indeed I do not think it very likely that they would ever have plucked up their courage to take a shot at Glubb Pasha or anyone else.

A few days later I received orders that I was to go with Saoud Rashdan to see General Cooke, who was inspecting a camp in the Jordan Valley. I naturally wondered what this summons might portend, but none of my guesses were anywhere near the right answer. The General took us aside and said that information had been received from some agent that Haj Ameen had put my name on his short list of persons to be bumped off. Apparently Glubb Pasha and Haza'a Majali also figured on this list, so I was in good company. I had in fact received this piece of information earlier. The Pasha had said that he had been on the list for a long time and in any case had his bodyguard, but it seems that he thought the Mufti's men had a better chance of getting me! The General turned to Saoud Rashdan and ordered him in the most solemn tones to see that wherever I went in future I had two bodyguards with me. "I hold you responsible."

Whether this report was fact or fiction I cannot say. Saoud Rashdan thought the agent had invented the whole story so as to earn his salary, and was highly entertained by it. My Adjutant had chosen a corporal called Ahmed Irhayel to command the section on guard at my house. This man was from Khdayer's own tribe, the Shammar of Iraq, and was a very strict N.C.O., who had been for some time one of Glubb Pasha's bodyguard. He was one of those whom I had myself selected for promotion in November 1953; and maybe this accounted for his diligence in protecting me! By night he continually prowled round the house inspecting his sentries, and if strangers visited us he always used to search them for concealed weapons. He regarded our haderi neighbours in Rafidia with the gravest suspicion. Ahmed Irhayel selected as his second-in-command one Salim Thahir, a tall Belgawi lance-corporal who had just returned from a P.T. course, and seemed to spend much of his time doing hand-stands, or teaching the rest of the men the extraordinary feats so dear to all rubber men. The rest of the guard were survivors from the original section that came from 4 Company in December, Abdulla Noman being one, or men selected by me or Ahmed Irhayel from our past experience of them. Abdulla Salameh had won the Gallantry Medal in Jerusalem, and Awwad Fweran had shown diligence during the Ajlun troubles. They were a good lot; always inviting me to tea in their tent, and I enjoyed their company. Once a week I used to inspect them, but usually our contacts were purely social. One afternoon we spent some time piling stones on the roof ready to throw at the rioters next time they should visit Hackett-Payne! The bedouin, like most shepherds I suppose, are great slingers and stone throwers. Once they practised scaling the rough stone walls of the house. Habash Daham and Salim Thahir were best at this game; they could reach the roof without any pause. At other times I used to teach them some of the unarmed combat tricks we learnt in the Commandos.

Ahmed Irhayel was a martinet and no man could go down into Nablus without his written pass!

"Le Printemps rapelie aux armes," and it was not disgruntled National Guardsmen, or Haj Ameen that were at this time uppermost in our minds. The Brigadier and I were chiefly concerned in the month that remained to us with putting the finishing touches to our defences. When we eventually left Jiftlik we hoped we were done with internal security for a time.

I re-read the intelligence summaries to refresh my memory as to the layout of the Israeli army and pondered over their possible lines of advance if the armistice, now nearly eight years old, should dissolve in a shooting war. It was highly improbable that there would be any major move before the end of March, but thereafter anything might happen. If the Egyptians were rearming the process would take them some time, but it seemed possible that by say July they would have become familiar with their new equipment, and given the users the necessary instruction. It might be, therefore, that the Israelis would consider the period between the end of March and the beginning of July a good time to strike.

With the Arab Legion at Latroun and Qalqilya, and with their own capital in Jerusalem, it might be that the Jews would feel bound to attack Jordan first. Yet the major incidents of recent months had been in the Gaza area, and so perhaps the Egyptians would take the first knock. Despite the respectful withdrawal of our forces from the Canal Zone the British officers of the Arab Legion had no exaggerated idea of the prowess of the Egyptian army. It was calculated that it ought to be able to hold out against the Israelis for a time, but I do not recall precisely whether the time was three days or four. My own opinion was, and is, that the Egyptians could do better than that, for after all their army had probably been overhauled since 1948, and they were not up against a first-class military power. But, whether or not the Egyptians were successful, it was certain that the Arab Legion would be in the forefront of the battle, either because Jordan herself had been attacked, or because she had gone to the assistance of Egypt. It was inconceivable that any Jordan Government, even should it wish to, could succeed in sitting on the fence when once the armistice between Israel and Egypt was finally and irrevocably broken.

In Jordan itself unhappily the greatest prize and the most obvious target was Jerusalem. In the event of war it was only too likely that once again the Holy City would be the scene of heavy fighting, for there was no other objective nearly as attractive. In the North the narrow valleys leading into the Judean Hills are blocked by the strong stone-built towns of Tulkarm and Jenin. If the Israelis should penetrate to Nablus or even Jiftlik, such an advance would prove nothing. I was convinced that their main forces would be disposed to attack Jerusalem, cover Tel-Aviv, and to hold off the Egyptians. The defence of Galilee, Afule, Beisan and even Haifa would have to be left to reserve brigades, bolstered up with squadrons of Sherman tanks — 1943 vintage.

It looked as if the Israelis would have the initiative, but on a four-hundred-mile front they could not be strong everywhere. Their army of some twenty brigades, infantry and armoured, was probably uneven in quality, for the proportion of regular troops was small, perhaps the equivalent of three brigades. At the best we were not dealing with the Hermann Goering Division, and such regulars as there were would probably be used in the South or against Jerusalem.

With these considerations in mind it may be imagined that as I reconnoitred the by-ways of my district I was not thinking only in terms of defence or withdrawal. To the Arab soldier, bedouin or haderi, regular or National Guard, Palestinian or Transjordanian, the attack was the thing. Ask him to advance and he would go. Ask him to withdraw and as like as not he would say that the wicked British had sold the pass. The defeat of 1948 still rankles and burns in the heart of every Arab, for defeat it was whatever local triumphs there may have been. Those of the bedouin who come from afar may not feel this shame, but the rest do, and some, the Beersheba bedouin, were themselves victims of the 1948 debacle. Any withdrawal was bound to mean the loss of those National Guardsmen whose homes were abandoned. In a staff college the battalions move about the map like so many pawns on a chessboard, backwards and forwards according to the whim of the master mind. But would the National Guard Regiments do their stuff as pawns? Only, I imagined, so long as they agreed with the plan. These thoughts, and many more, wandered in and out of my mind as I rode round my sector in those February days. If we were to go back I reckoned we had better wait till we were shoved, and said so.

It need not be assumed from all this that a showdown was regarded as either inevitable or desirable. Seconded British officers were commissioned as brigade, battalion and squadron commanders in the service of an allied foreign power, whose enemies were our enemies for as long as we remained in Jordan. We were to that extent like the mercenaries of former days, the conditions of service were good or we would not have stayed. The possibility of a war with Israel was just an occupational hazard.

Spring came early with almond blossoms and fruit trees to beautify each little valley of the land of Samaria. Every morning as I drove to work I passed Sebastiyye, the ancient capital, standing back from the road like a hill town in Italy. Sometimes from the hills above on a clear day we could see Mount Hermon, the Jebel esh Sheikh, far away in Syria like a cloud in the northern sky, for only its snowclad peak was visible.

I had two rifle companies in reserve now, 1 and 4, and Musayeb had already begun to train the pick of both for the Arab Legion Day Parade. He was as smart as ever but he had gone sour. I realized now that he had been malingering in January to avoid being involved in duties which might damage his popularity. I ran him up in front of the Brigadier for failing to comply with the Adjutant's orders, and for misusing government transport. He got well bitten for his pains and did not like it. Next day when I was visiting his camp he told me that if I was always displeased with him he could not work and became sick, to which I replied that I had not forgotten the many good things he had done for the Regiment, but that he should have stayed at duty during the troubles. I should not have been surprised had he asked to be transferred to another regiment after these blunt words, but he did not do so, and having treated his wounds with a reminder of his undeniable achievements in the past I left him.

General Cooke and Colonel Luard paid us a visit towards the end of the month. In their honour Fuad organized the best mensif I ever tasted, with chickens as well as sheep. The Brigadier and several of the National Guard battalion commanders were among the guests. After lunch we drove to Tubas and admired the interesting monuments in the valley there.

Another day I was summoned to Brigade to meet a bevy of Arab officers who had come down for some lecture or conference. Besides Ali Hiyari and Sadiq Shara' there was a slim young lieutenant-colonel whom I had not seen before, though I guessed who it might be. I asked Sadiq this officer's name. It was Ali Abu Nawar. Of average height, dark-haired and with regular features, he cut a very presentable figure. They were all full of smiles that morning, and not least the returned exile, who, confident and self-assured, treated the two full colonels as equals. Well he might.

The sands were running out now. In a little more than a month Arthur Green would be going on three months' leave and it had been arranged that I should take over the brigade until July, when I was to return to the British army. My successor designate, Major Irshaid Mershoud, arrived from 1 Regiment and I began to hand over to him. He spoke reasonable English and, although I would rather have left the Regiment to Saoud Rashdan, I found Irshaid very agreeable to work with, and keen to learn.

I was getting used to the idea of leaving. One morning I climbed the hill above El Fandagoumiye to watch a demonstration of a platoon attack. The men sat on rocks under a great tree while Muhamad Moazi lectured them. It was a lovely morning and I wandered away, looking down on the little hamlet, where some of the officers and N.C.O.s hired quarters, and away across the fields and olive groves to the Plain of Sanur, now a lake after the winter rains. The whole country was vividly green. Looking back, the shemaghs of the bedouin under their tree made a great splash of colour. Above on the hillside, lithe and nimble, the attackers stalked forward, slipping from boulder to boulder, alert and dashing even on training. It seemed a pity to be leaving it all.

When we were at Zeraq in January another British officer had given me a translation of a remarkable document which had come into his hands:

Pamphlet No. 36, issued by the Arab Legion Liberal Officers' Rally.
In the Name of God, the Compassionate, the Merciful.

In this pamphlet we go back to review recent incident, in our country, which have been unveiled by the C.G.S. imposed upon us, i.e. General Glubb. We refer to the crimes perpetrated on our brothers... who refused to accept the adherence of Jordan to Colonialist Pacts and the Majali Family Pact. This was expected, after Glubb had taken preliminary action by lecturing various units. This was also demonstrated by his desire to establish stores for the British Army and for the U.S.A, in different parts of our country, such as Mafraq, Khaw, Azraq area and Aqaba, in order to make our Legion the 'Protective shield' to guard these stores for them and quit our first and last target, which is to destroy the pet of the Colonialists, Israel.

Do you know, brethren, the proposals of General Templer, who is called 'The Tiger of Malay' and who was found to be nothing but a mouse. Here they are. He wants to establish:

1. A new brigade H.Q., with the usual services, medical, signals and transport.

2. Two infantry regiments with their 17-pounders, 3-inch mortars and normal small-arms.

3. Reformation and armament of one brigade with armoured cars and Comet tanks.

These are the arms which 'The Mouse of Jordan' wants to supply us with, in return for binding the life of this Legion to the wheel of the British command. He knows that these arms, especially the tanks, have not been used since World War II, and are sold as scrap iron in Britain. Meanwhile they provide Israel with the latest weapons of destruction such as Centurion tanks in order to let her repeat her aggression on us, and massacres such as Deir Yassin and Qibya. British financial aid to Jordan, it has been agreed, will be replaced by brother Arab States collectively, should Britain cease to pay it.

The pamphlet goes on to allege that the British subsidy is spent on paying British officers at excessive rates. It continues:

The National Guardsman who guards our frontiers, and stands ready for any emergency with his rifle and only 25 rounds... gets only JD 1.900 fils a month to support himself and his family, which may not be less than seven persons.

Are we to remain subject to the will of this old Glubb and his director of C.I.D., Patrick Coghill?

He began to feel that his existence was uncertain after his failure to carry out his conspiracy to make us sign the pact with Turkey. Therefore he began to torture our brother Liberal Officers and to send them to prison. This is only achieved by virtue of his tails the traitor officers like Qaid Abdul Rahman Sahen, Khaled es Sahen, and the director of his terrorism, Muhamad Suheimat.

We will not keep silent under these circumstances and will stand by our people against Colonialist Pacts. The day on which the gallows will be erected to hang these traitors will come soon and it is not too far.

We appeal to His Majesty, the youthful King Hussein, the supreme commander of the Arab Legion, to meddle [sic] in this affair, to refuse any Colonialist Pact, wherever it may come from, and to accept the financial aid that was offered by the Arab States in order to get rid of these red-faced people from Jordan.

Another round will follow.

The Liberal Officers' Rally.

When I saw this pamphlet I was deeply involved in the suppression of the January outbreak, nevertheless I gave it a certain amount of thought. I had known since the summer of 1954 of the existence of the Young Officers' Movement and this was clearly the same thing. It seemed to me that if discontent existed it must be among the intelligentsia — the artillery and the engineers. Still, it was disturbing to think that there was a body of officers in the Legion, sufficiently ill-disposed or muddle-headed to put out pamphlets of this sort, containing as propaganda often does a grain of truth in a bushel of lies.

And what of 9 Regiment? They had done well enough at Salt and Ajlun, but some at least had not cared for operating in Zerqa. It was too near home. Every battalion in every army has in its ranks a few of those so aptly described by the Americans as "weak sisters". I reckoned there were not many left in 9, and that Saoud and I had a pretty good idea who they were. In fact, in February 1956, the Regiment was better than it had ever been. We had a strong team of company commanders, backed by some first-class platoon leaders. Most of the duds had gone.

And on 1st March, the youthful King Hussein did as he was bidden.

On this evening, for the first time in months, I went to the Cinema. The party consisted of my wife, Mr. and Mrs. Elias Salfiti and the British Vice-Consul in Nablus, Jackie Hackett Payne. I am sorry to say that I disobeyed orders and left my bodyguard at home. I also forgot to mention where I was going. The film was *Desirée*. We had barely sat through a wrongful arrest and a coup d'état or two, when someone loomed up and said that Qaid Young was wanted below. There I found the Brigadier's driver Lutfi, who took me to his house, my conscience pricking me somewhat, since I knew that he could only have found me by detective work which must have taken some time.

As we drove up Arthur Green opened the front door.

"Come in. Something's happening. Glubb is out."

My comment is unprintable. I accepted a whisky and soda, and heard that Brigadiers Galletly and Hutton, Sir Patrick Coghill, Lt.-Cols. Grey and Griffiths had also been relieved of their commands.

There was a direct line to the H.Q. of 1 Brigade which for some reason had not been cut. Brigadier Galletly himself had phoned through this information. It was impossible to get through to the General.

"We're still in. Can't understand it, can you?"

"I suppose they're not afraid of us."

The telephone rang. I heard Arthur say, "I don't take bloody orders from Mazin Ajlouni." I joined him by the telephone. After a short talk he hung up.

"Abdel Kerim Dabbas has got to go and take over command of 5 Regiment," he said. The officer in question was second-in-command of 6 Regiment. He had not previously been considered a potential battalion commander.

We had another whisky and soda. It was not long before the telephone rang again. There was a short conversation.

"Suleiman Masoud's out. Mahmoud Moussa's getting command of the Hashemite Regiment."

"Good God!"

Mahmoud Moussa was the officer who had been in command of 4 Regiment when we relieved them at Jerusalem in 1954.

We returned to the drawing-room and went on with our drinks.

A few minutes passed before the telephone rang a third time. The Brigadier walked back into the hall, and I followed him.

"It's Ali Hiyari," he said. There was a bit of talk, then he beamed at me: "You're out," he said. It was like being given l.b.w. in a cricket match.

"And what about me?" asked the Brigadier. There was a little more talk. As he put down the receiver, he said: "I am to remain in command for the time being. I wonder how long that will be. Salameh Etayek is being sent to take over from you."

Although by this time I expected to be relieved of my command, I was incensed at having to hand over to Salameh, whom I considered had been disloyal. We returned to the drawing-room, and sat for a while discussing what had happened.

"It's His Majesty's orders. There's nothing we can do about it," said the Brigadier. We had another drink, and then I asked if I might send for my second-in-command and Adjutant, as I thought they might be upset. I went home and rang up the Regiment. Before Saoud arrived, I tried to ring up General

Cooke to satisfy myself that the orders were genuine. I was surprised to get through, but it was Brigadier Hutton who answered.

"Yes, the orders are perfectly genuine. These are His Majesty's orders. All these changes of personnel are to go through. It only remains for you to give whoever is taking over from you as good a handover as possible, and then come over here with your family...."

A Land-Rover arrived. I heard the sentry's challenge, "Min", and heard Saoud reply. Khdayer was with him, both of them wrapped up in their greatcoats. I told them what had happened and what I had heard from Jim Hutton. They were stunned. We discussed the situation for a time, and I reminded them that I held a commission from King Hussein ...

In the early hours I was woken by the telephone: Salameh had wasted no time in arriving. He asked if I had any orders for him. I told him to go to bed, and that I would hand over to him next day.

When I arrived at R.H.Q. everything was perfectly normal. I went up to the office, and after a little talk asked Saoud and Khdayer to leave Salameh alone with me.

"Sorry about this," he said.

"Oh, that's all right, I was handing over next month in any case."

"Anyway, I know you would rather hand over to me than anyone else," he said.

"I always told you that you would be a Qaid one day."

"I did not want it like this."

"When did you know about it?"

"About what? About the Pasha? I was sent for to Qiada about nine o'clock last night, and Radi Ennab — you know the

Zaim — told me. It had to be, you know. The Pasha is an old man now."

I began collecting up my books and papers. David Smith came on the telephone about something. I asked him to get me an aeroplane.

"You do not want to stay on?" asked Salameh.

I explained as clearly as possible, but without heat I trust, that if I was behaving myself nicely that was not to say that I was prepared to stay on, after being relieved of my command without any reason being given.

I spent several hours clearing up my papers.

I told Salameh that I proposed, if he had no objection, to keep the guard at my house.

"The whole Regiment is yours," he replied. It was all loving kindness, and before I departed he said that he wished to make a mensif before I went.

In the afternoon we drove to visit Jerusalem. I ran into Lt.-Col. Muhamad Ishaq, whom I had known well in 1954. He was still chief military member of the Jordan delegation to the Mixed Armistice Committee. He was cheerful and friendly and gave no sign that he was in any way surprised at what had occurred. After a few minutes' talk we said goodbye to each other. As he shook hands he said: "Whatever has happened now, we will never forget what you did for us in the Jerusalem incident."

The next few days were hectic. Troops of our neighbours were in and out of the house offering the smallest prices they could think of for our furniture, or as often as not, merely fingering the goods. First it was announced that the Arab Legion would buy the furniture of the officers who had been relieved. Then Karim Ohan, keen to show his loyalty to the Movement, decided that would be illegal. This was no more than I had expected, and eventually everything, even our car and the refrigerator, was sold. The officers of 2 Brigade H.Q. were as charming and helpful as ever. Several of them came to visit me. Carpenters were sent to crate our baggage, and stencil addresses on it, and by 6th March we had packed up and were ready to go. I was permitted to keep the Land-Rover, and Salameh sent me a 3-tonner to take our baggage to Zerqa.

Brigadier Green was still in command of 2 Brigade. Without his being consulted two of his commanding officers, Suleiman Masoud and myself, had been relieved of their commands. Neither he nor I felt particularly worked up about my own case for I was leaving in July; but it seemed a bit hard on Suleiman, who was a loyal old soul. Arthur Green felt this deeply, and so one night he rang up the General and said he wished to resign. The officers of brigade headquarters had a charming arrangement with their signallers by which his conversations were relayed to their mess, and this news spread like wildfire, causing considerable surprise. They could not conceive how a British officer could bring himself to give up a good job and decent allowances merely upon a point of principle.

I did not go out to the Regiment again, not wishing it to be said that I had been trying to stir up trouble. Although the Regiment was in the line some of the officers and senior ranks were able to come and see me and say goodbye. Salameh Etayek, Saoud Rashdan, Khdayer, Said Saleh, Fuad, Ahmed Qasim and Urfan Johari all visited me before I left and in addition some of the officers from Brigade Headquarters.

Undoubtedly some of the officers were delighted to see the last of me! The malingering Musayeb said as much in the Officers' Mess, and Salameh Etayek did not think fit to check him. It was left to one of the company commanders, and he not the boldest in the ordinary way, to rebuke him. Mansour

Kreishan and Muhamad Rkheimeh were alleged to welcome this upheaval, presumably hoping for advancement. The former was a good officer who had always had my support; the latter, with his Egyptian upbringing, I had come to mistrust.

Undoubtedly the majority of the bedouin officers and men were profoundly disturbed by the departure of Glubb Pasha, whom they regarded as their father, and had they been called upon to resist his overthrow would have been prepared to do so by force of arms. This they were prevented from doing by their British commanders! The bedouin are mercenaries, and they are not on the whole impulsive people or prone to act on the spur of the moment. If they are in doubt or feel wronged they will brood over things, and discuss them among themselves for a time before acting. Even so, by the end of May, over a thousand bedouin had departed from the Legion, including a hundred each from the two armoured car regiments, and the 1st Infantry Regiment. They have been told that there is no difference between haderi and bedu. This they may not believe. Many of their senior officers, including Suleiman Irteimeh and Zaal Irhayel, have been sent to the National Guard, which, however unfairly, is despised by the bedouin. It is no wonder if they are trickling away. Being generous people they are very inclined to lend out all their money! Many of those who still remain are probably only waiting to collect their debts.

On 6th March, we left Nablus for Zerqa, where once more we inflicted ourselves on the long-suffering Smiths. The atmosphere in Zerqa was tense, quite unlike that of Nablus, where the coup had been received fairly quietly. In Zerqa we really felt that we were living on a volcano and the morale of the few bedouin who had come with me from Nablus wilted like a waterless flower. Juma'a alone was unmoved by the atmosphere of hostility which prevailed; he cared for no man. To make matters worse Habash Daham, a dependable old soldier, developed raging toothache. I had already sent Ahmed Irhayel, Thiab Hamdan and Awwad Fweran back to their companies, and only some of the younger soldiers remained. As soon as I could get rid of my heavy baggage I sent the others away, retaining only Juma'a and Abdulla Heikal.

The evening passed pleasantly in discussing the events of the 1st, the reactions of our acquaintances, British and Arab, and in speculating about the future. Between ten and eleven we turned in, but before I could get into bed the telephone rang. Nobody answered it and so, presuming that David had fallen asleep, I went. It was General Cooke.

"Something is going on in the Armoured Car Lines, vehicles moving about and so on. Just let me know if anything passes your place."

I went back to our room and began to dress. The Armoured Car Lines lay to the East of the General's house: almost immediately a vehicle shot past. Joan put out the light and we pulled one of the curtains back. An armoured car swung round the corner and dashed by, then another, followed by a Land-Rover. I told David what had happened, and then, not wishing to miss anything, I stuck my Luger under my arm and went to the General's house. It was quite dark and a breeze stirred the trees along the road. Although I was in civilian clothes, and did not know the password, I got past the sentries by saying that the General had sent for me.

I found him in his large airy drawing-room with Ski Galletly and a small dark man, whom I could not place, though as he had a moustache I took him to be an officer. Apparently nobody knew what was happening and that included Ali Hiyari, the Chief of Staff, who had said as much on the telephone. A little later Luard turned up, but he could add nothing to our information, except that the Camp Commandant, Idris Bey, was enjoying himself in the Mess. I talked for a while with the Brigadier, who had been replaced by his former D.A.Q.M.G., Ali Abu Nawar, and was not particularly pleased about it. To make matters worse he had had to leave his wife behind at his Headquarters near Jerusalem. "I told the servants that if anything happened to Gerry I would shoot them one by one … But I haven't even got a pistol." I said I thought I could produce one.

I went over to the stranger and asked him, "What part do you play in this military comedy?"

"I am an artist," he replied. John Norton had been touring Jordan painting the peasant types and soldiers of the Legion.

After a while Luard went over to the Mess and fetched Idris Bey, to see if he could throw any light on the manoeuvres of the Armoured Car Regiment. The Mess was not a hundred yards away and they soon arrived. Idris, who was in uniform, had not been drinking lime juice. He looked round unsteadily and greeted each of us effusively.

"Ah! My friend the Brigadier. My friend Young Bey! All my friends!" I got the impression that he expected to be beaten with a blunt instrument. We learned nothing of any interest from him, presumably because he knew nothing; so I suggested that the simplest thing might be to ring up the 1st Armoured Car Regiment and ask them what they were about. The General spoke to Naif Hadeed, the new C.O., who was quite forthcoming. He had received his orders from Ali Abu Nawar, the commander of the 1st Brigade, through Turki Hindawi, the C.O. of the Divisional Regiment, a curious chain of command, which by-passed the Headquarters of the Legion and the Division. When he had divulged this much the signaller on the exchange, who no doubt thought Naif Bey had said enough, put an end to the conversation. The object of the exercise remained obscure, and it was thought that Brigadier Mitford, the commander of the Armoured Brigade, might be able to cast some light upon it. Since we could not get him on the telephone, I walked round to his house, but he was out. I returned via Bet Smith, where I found David standing outside.

"They're all milling around in the Artillery Lines," he said, and looking away to the North we could see lights moving about. "You know those chaps you saw. Well, just after you left they dashed back again." With this meagre intelligence I returned to the General.

After a time Mitford, who had been in Amman, appeared, somewhat incensed at having been held up at a road block, where a sergeant of 1st Armoured Car Regiment was in charge.

We went to bed not much the wiser. If anyone knew what was going on it was Ali Abu Nawar, who for reasons best known to himself, had ordered out 1st Armoured Car Regiment and 2nd Field Regiment to surround Zerqa cantonment. In the days that followed some said that the intention had been to arrest Abdel Rahman es Sahen; while others named Sadiq Shara' and his brother Saleh as the intended victims. An impression lingered that perhaps all was not well in the ranks of the Young Officers' Movement.

To one brought up on British notions of how the chain of command should work, it seemed strange that the commander of a brigade in Palestine, without consulting his divisional commander, should call out troops of two other brigades, without telling his fellow brigadiers, in order to arrest officers who certainly did not belong to his command. It was evident that the young officers had their Headquarters on the West Bank, with a branch at Zerqa. It was not Major General Radi

Ennab, the new C.G.S., nor even Colonel Ali Hiyari, the Chief of Staff; but Ali Abu Nawar, still a mere Lt.-Colonel, who was revealed as the man of the hour.

On 12th March, I visited Qiada to make the final arrangements for my departure. Although I was in civilian clothes I had no difficulty in getting in, Juma'a did not stop, and I merely waved my identity card at the sentries.

I saw a number of people I knew, Karim Ohan, Bob Young, and a lieutenant called Ahmed Khadra, one of the few people who still found time for his routine work, dealt with our passports. Jim Hutton was going round the various offices saying goodbye to the staff officers.

While I was waiting for the passports, I went to take my leave of Ali Hiyari, who was sitting in his office with two civilians. "This had to come," he said, and then as I left, "We will never forget what you did in the Jerusalem incident."

Before I left, one officer who had better be nameless, came up and shook me warmly by the hand and said; "Our best regards to our previous master."

My next call was at an insurance agent's, where I found myself talking to one of the men who had been with Ali. I could not help wondering whether perhaps the Colonel thought it time to take out some life insurance!

We left Amman airport on 13th March, and flew to London. Numbers of British officers and their wives were there to see the plane off. We stood around talking until it was time to go. It was a cheerful gathering. Last of all I said goodbye to Abdulla Heikal and to Juma'a.

CHAPTER XI: CONSEQUENCES

There have been considerable changes in the personnel of the Arab Legion, even since the night of 1st March. Major General Radi Ennab did not long enjoy the honours which to do him justice he had probably not sought, and Ali Abu Nawar, having advanced from Major to Major-General in six months, now reigns in his stead. It was reported at the same time that the new C.G.S. had said recently that Sir John Glubb had "deliberately centralised all military and political power in Jordan in his own person", and had been "the worst enemy to Anglo-Jordan understanding". He said that the military mission which had visited Egypt had rejected "a genuine financial offer", because Jordan wished to retain her close ties with Britain and the financial assistance for which in return Britain was given bases there.

Colonel Sadiq Shara' succeeded Ali Abu Nawar as Chief of Staff. Ali Hiyari is G.O.C. of 1st Division; Fawwaz Maher and Radi Hindawi have infantry brigades. All these, save the' last, have commanded battalions and all have now been promoted brigadier. Colonel Izzat Hassan, the former C.O. of 6 Regiment is now a brigade commander. The Artillery is commanded by Brigadier Muhamad Ma'ayta, whose recent appointments have been a succession of police districts. With his experience he should be able to keep his officers' minds on their gunnery, and away from politics. All these officers were until recently senior to Ali Abu Nawar, and, if they are human, must occasionally feel doubts as to whether they really deserved to be passed over by him.

The armoured arm is now commanded by a more junior officer, a graduate of the Staff College at Camberley, who replaced Mahmoud Rousan.

Lt.-Col. Karim Ohan has come to London as military attaché, leaving his new post of Quartermaster General to Lt.-Col. Jubran Hawa, the commander of the Supply and Transport service. Jubran was so highly thought of that he was the first Arab to take over a senior appointment from a British officer.

Ali Hiyari, Sadiq Shara' and Fawwaz Maher were all destined for high rank in due course. They are now in their mid-thirties, and there seems no reason why they should not rise to the occasion merely because they have had greatness thrust upon them a little earlier than expected. The weakness is lower down at battalion level, but with one notable exception it can be said that Jordan is now fielding her 1st eleven.

Transjordan was the only sovereign state in the Middle East whose soldiers fought for the allies, serving outside their own country practically throughout the last war. In the year that followed the fall of France the Arab Legion fought beside the British, at a time when we were practically without allies.

In the days before 1948 no country in the Middle East was more peaceful and secure than Transjordan in the days when King Abdulla and Glubb Pasha ruled the land in feudal or rather patriarchal fashion. In Turkish times it had been a peaceful enough province, but now it was properly administered as well. The fighting in Palestine, the flood of refugees and the murder of King Abdulla in 1951 have changed all that.

Now the Communists are active in Jordan as in every Middle Eastern country, and have made numerous converts among the refugees. But Egyptian influence is supreme. It is not without significance that when he was in Paris Ali Abu Nawar was often seen in the company of Colonel Sarawat Okacha, the Egyptian military attaché. And now Said el Mufti wishes to amend the Treaty of Alliance: Colonel Nasser, who has long strained every nerve to weaken British influence in Jordan, would like to see the Treaty revoked entirely. One sometimes wonders whether that would be a disadvantage.

Since 1946 Britain has paid Jordan £75,000,000 mostly in grants. Total payments to Jordan for the financial year 1956-7 are at the rate of £12,550,000 a year of which £9,200,000 is for the Legion. The taxpayer would presumably be glad to save this money in the future, particularly if he felt that he was getting nothing in return.

It is true, however, that the British army has a garrison at Aqaba and an armoured car regiment stationed at Ma'an, besides various ordnance depots, all of which would presumably have to be moved if the treaty were abrogated. Similarly the Royal Air Force has bases at Amman and Mafraq.

At present we British are rather like a man backing both horses in the Palestine Stakes where there are only two runners. When Miss Golda Meyerson recently became Foreign Minister of Israel one of her first acts was to thank Great Britain for the gift of two destroyers.

At least we are impartial. We issue gunpowder and match to both sides with most admirable magnanimity. It merely remains to wait for the Bang!

Whatever we wanted when we built up the Legion it would be a grave error if we were to imagine that the Arabs regard it as anything but an instrument of revenge against the Israelis. Whether, if war broke out again, the Arabs would be the winners is another question. At his best the Arab soldier is not unlike the British, for he has a sense of humour and is tough and hardy. But while there is no reason to doubt his dash in the attack, the question remains whether in defence, under continuous pounding, he would show the same dogged qualities that we look for and admire in our own men. The Arab Legion, with its small corps of British officers, was turning into a disciplined, steady force, fit for any form of warfare from the sudden raid so dear to the Arab heart to a straightforward slogging match. The Arab officers are, many of them, skilful and determined soldiers, but, through no fault of their own, they have no experience of modern war. Many of them have been in action, but the conditions in Palestine were not those of Alamein or Normandy.

Later in 1956 the Legion was not the same force it was in February. Courts martial, dismissals and desertions hardly make for confidence. Should they have the second round with the Israelis for which they are seemingly so eager, one wonders whether the Arabs will make a better showing than they did in 1948. For if the Jeish distinguished itself then, the people as a whole evidently did not.

Miss Coate tells us that:

"In 1948 it proved useless to expostulate with the village youths of Transjordan, who would rush off in large bands down to the Jordan valley to help, as they said, with the fighting and, after confusing the issue by getting tangled up with the regular forces, would come home again as soon as they had collected as much loot as they could carry. 'After all,' said one woman, 'who would want to get killed?'"

The resentment of the British, Parliament, Press and Public alike, was aroused by the black and midnight way in which the Young Officers' Movement struck at Glubb Pasha. Why all the secrecy? Why not just say "You no longer enjoy our confidence. Pray submit your resignation". But the Liberal Officers, after five years of underground plotting, were far too tortuous minded to suppose that the Pasha would depart without a murmur. Their guilty consciences told them that if the blow was not struck by stealth they would all find themselves in a concentration camp. Absurd as this seems, it was their belief.

To understand what has happened, and is still happening, one must try to see what the Jordanians are thinking. But this is extremely difficult for a Westerner. Alan Moorehead, in a passage about Constantinople before the Turks came into the war of 1914,[17] has an apt and illuminating phrase: "In Constantinople this false and artificial excitement was all the more intense since no one really knew the rules of the game, and in the uncertain jigsaw of ideas which is created by any meeting between the East and the West no one could ever look more than a move or two ahead." That is precisely the trouble in Amman in 1956. Nobody really knows the rules.

Certain newspapers wrote of Jordan's folly, ingratitude and even insolence, in dismissing Sir John Glubb and the rest of us. But such talk does less than nothing towards a proper understanding of the situation. Great Britain and Jordan are allies because they considered it to their mutual advantage to sign a Treaty. If they have received seventy-five millions of our money, they believe that they also have to thank us for the Palestine Problem.

The rules really are different. For example the Arab conception of loyalty is different to ours: first and foremost he owes loyalty to his own family, and in his view this comes before loyalty to his Regiment or to his Country. That is not to say that these last ideas have not taken root, Western plants

---

[17] Alan Moorehead, *Gallipoli*, p. 13.

though they are. Again to the Arab nepotism comes naturally; something which we regard as shameful is to him a sacred duty. To speak of corruption is to misunderstand the depths of his loyalty to his family. Loyalty to the religious community is strong, and is equally marked among the Armenian, Circassian and Christian Arab sects.

Islam is still, to most Arabs, a stronger force than Nationalism, but the one embraces the other, for whoever else may forget it, they remember that their ancestors carved out an Empire. It is not for nothing that the Jordanian Orders of Chivalry are called: "Renaissance" and "Independence." Dislike, even hatred, of the "patronizing, dominating foreigner" is as natural to the Jordanian of today as to the Turk of 1914.

Arabs believe that Western foreigners regard them as backward and uncivilized. If they do they wrong them, for nobody has more admiration for the marvels of modern science than the Arab. It is left to the English to admire the primitive charm of the Jordanian countryside, the wooden ploughs, the camels, the gaily dressed woman carrying water-jars miraculously balanced on their heads. The educated Arab admires the Packard and saves up to buy a radio. Once in Beirut I was hotly assailed by a smart young Arab in a suit of European style, who saw me trying to take photographs of people in their traditional peasant costume. He thought that I would show it to people at home and deride the Lebanese as barbarians, while I thought the old-fashioned dresses were picturesque and beautiful.

It should not be difficult for a Briton to appreciate the longing of Jordanians to be masters in their own house. Foreign aid and tutelage galls them. Few indeed thank Point 4 or the World Health Organization for their good work in the land; they merely resent the cruel lot which makes them dependent on money from abroad. Jordan is a young state, and just as her twenty-one-year-old King resented the tutelage of a General of fifty-eight, the nation resents the guidance of more well-established nations.

This is not to say that Jordanians resent the guidance of Egypt, the self-appointed leader of the Arab world. Colonel Nasser's high-handed action in "nationalizing" the Suez Canal was nowhere more loudly applauded than in Jordan. Had the Legion at that time, as formerly, been firmly under the control of a corps of British officers, Nasser would have expected but little support from that quarter.

If the Arab's loyalty is to his family, his gratitude is to God. The refugee, existing on a United Nations dole in Karameh, will mutter "God is generous". He will thank no man, for God is the Giver. Nor does it help to speak of ingratitude. The rules are different.

If by some strange chance the United Nations should decide to restore the land of Palestine to the people who owned it in 1918; and if by some still stranger chance they carried through this plan, it would be to hear the Arabs praise God for returning them to their country. Rightly or wrongly, no credit would go to Man.

A NOTE ON THE LEGION WE KNEW

The Arab Legion was formed in 1920 by Captain F. G. Peake, and was originally about one thousand strong, consisting of two squadrons of cavalry, two infantry companies, a troop of artillery and a signals section. Its title, Al Jeish al Arabi, means The Arab Army, and was that given to the force created in the First World War by the Amir Feisal and Colonel Lawrence. Peake, commanding the Egyptian Camel Corps, had served alongside Feisal's men.

The Transjordan Frontier Force, a body of British Imperial troops raised a few years later, was entirely separate, and came under the command of the High Commissioner for Palestine. The Arab Legion was and is the army of an independent state allied to Great Britain.

The Desert Patrol, recruited from among the bedouin, was formed by Glubb Pasha in 1931, to put an end to raiding, the age-old pastime of the nomadic tribesmen. As Glubb Pasha wrote: "the bedouins' chief pleasure in life is to bear arms, and the simultaneous abolition of raiding drove the most gallant and enterprising young men into the service." How the ninety bedouin soldiers of the Desert Patrol suppressed raiding, without bloodshed, is a tale already told by the Pasha himself.[18]

In 1936 the Arabs of Palestine revolted against the mandatory government, and there was grave danger that the trouble might spread to Transjordan. At this time the Legion, including police, numbered no more than one thousand two hundred men, scattered about the country in small

---

[18] *The Story of the Arab Legion.*

detachments. Two additional cavalry squadrons and three hundred and fifty bedouin lorried infantry were raised as a reserve.

In March 1939 a big gang, about a hundred strong, entered Transjordan from Syria, making for the wooded mountains of Ajlun, but within a few days they were broken up with the loss of over thirty killed and wounded. The Legion had five casualties, including one of its three British officers, Lieutenant Macadam, who was killed. There were incidents at Tafila and elsewhere, but generally the gangs tried to establish themselves in Ajlun district. During March and April they were continually harried — and eventually destroyed by two cavalry squadrons and the Desert Mechanized Force. Good weapon training and the will to push on night and day did the trick, and the rebels failed to get going in Transjordan. Actions such as that at Beit Idis in April were wonderful training for what lay ahead.

On 21st March 1939, Glubb Pasha assumed command on the retirement of Colonel Peake. When the Second World War broke out the Amir Abdulla placed all the resources of Transjordan at the disposal of Great Britain, and after the fall of France it was evident that every man would be needed. General Wavell visited Amman, was received by His Highness, and reviewed a troop of the Desert Mechanized Force on Merka airfield. It was agreed that the Jeish should be doubled, and that the British Army would provide weapons and equipment. When the fighting began in the Western Desert the Amir offered to send a contingent to the front. In reply he was asked to provide a company to guard an important aerodrome in Palestine. Two hundred infantry were collected for this purpose and given the title of the 1st Infantry Company of the Arab Legion.

In April 1941, after the pro-Axis coup in Baghdad, the Iraqi Army besieged the Royal Air Force cantonment at Habbaniya. The Desert Mechanized Regiment was the advanced guard of the relief force, and fought in all the operations which led to the capture of Baghdad in May.

Next came the invasion of Syria, in which the same Regiment took part in the attack on Palmyra and won the spirited action at Sukhna (29th June) where the French lost eleven killed, eighty prisoners, six armoured cars, twelve machine-guns and four trucks, their 2nd Light Desert Company being destroyed. Thanks to their speed and dash the Arab Legion lost only one man killed and one wounded.

Not long afterwards the 1st Regiment was completed, then 2nd and 3rd Regiments were raised, and a brigade headquarters was formed. The target became six regiments. Ford truck chassis were imported from the United States, and on them the Legion built armoured cars to its own design. Hundreds of the bedouin poured into the training camp at Azraq. But as ill luck would have it the Jeish took no further part in the campaigns of the Second World War, and was not in action again until in 1948 Great Britain gave up the Palestine mandate. Then it bore the brunt of the fighting with the Israelis which followed; for it was the Legion that defended the Old City of Jerusalem, by far the most important success achieved by the forces of the Arab League. In the successful defence of Latroun, the capture of Radar and the fighting round Bab-el-Wad, the Jeish showed itself more than a match for the Israeli levies, and when the Egyptian front broke it was left to the Legion to save Hebron.

1949 saw the beginning of a period of rapid expansion. The 1st Division was formed, consisting of three infantry brigades, each supported by its own field regiment. A light anti-aircraft regiment was raised, and an armoured brigade with two armoured car regiments and a regiment of self-propelled anti-tank guns. Besides engineers the usual base services for supplies, repairs, transport and ordnance came into being. The Police force remained an integral part of the Legion, consisting of cavalry and infantry for the settled areas; and camelry for the desert. The latter are bedouin, and still wear the uniform of the original Desert Patrol.

There is now a small Royal Jordanian Air Force, which consists of a communications flight, an air observation flight, and a training wing of Vampire aircraft.

There is in addition a flotilla for patrolling the Dead Sea, commanded until recently by Major Douglas, formerly of the Royal Marines, commonly known as the Dead Sea Lord.

Up until 1st March there were sixty-four British officers serving in Jordan, about sixteen on contract, and the remainder seconded from the British Army. This is not a book about the British officers, but I do not think it is going too far to say, en passant, that they were a reasonably strong team. All of them, seconded and contract officers, held King Hussein's commission, and those of the 1st Division were ordered by General Cooke on 5th January 1956, to have their commissions framed and hung in their offices, so as to make it clear to one and all that they were just as much members of the Legion as anyone else. The organization, training and equipment was on British lines, and the Legion was, and is, financed by grants from the Foreign Office and the War Office, amounting to some nine million pounds a year.

The Arab Legion is backed by a number of reservists and by the National Guard, which is composed entirely of infantry regiments. It has a sprinkling of regular officers and N.C.O.s, and is not unlike a cross between our Territorial Army and the Home Guard. It is well-armed on conventional lines, and most regiments have been called up for considerable periods of training. The National Guard is financed from the. British subsidy with some help from the Jordan Government and with occasional gifts from other members of the Arab League.

In 1953 the 1st Division had only one brigade stationed on the West Bank of the Jordan, and the remainder of the Division was training on the East Bank. Since the Qibya incident in October 1953 the Jordanian Government has always had to keep two brigades in Palestine to observe the Israelis.

The camelry of the Desert Patrol, the Desert Reconnaissance Squadron and seven regiments are bedouin; the regiments in question being the 1st, 2nd, 3rd, 7th and 9th Infantry and the 1st and 2nd Armoured Cars. The rest of the Arab Legion are haderi. In the next note I have occasion to write more about the bedouin, but here it may be appropriate to say something of the personnel of haderi regiments. They are drawn from the towns and villages of Palestine and Transjordan, and represent the settled inhabitants of the town as opposed to the nomadic dwellers in the desert. It may be argued that basically both haderi and bedouin spring from the same stock. Perhaps it may be that waves of bedouin have moved in from the desert, century after century, have settled down, and becoming farmers have gradually been absorbed by the original inhabitants of the town. It may be, though physical appearances are against this theory. The dark, lithe bedouin of Iraq or the Nejd are very different in appearance to the corn-fed countrymen of Kerak or Qalqilya. The Franks, in Crusading times or even later days, would seem to have left their progeny in Palestine, if fair hair and blue eyes mean anything. The haderi infantryman is a good, solid, well-behaved soldier, with the virtues of his fellahin ancestry. The officers, who are reasonably well educated, are as a body too sophisticated and comfort loving, though there are many good leaders among them. In general the more highly educated officers are to be found in the engineers, the artillery and the divisional anti-tank regiment. Some of them have shown themselves to be highly efficient: it remains to be seen whether they will devote themselves to their profession to the exclusion of politics.

The haderi Arab is excellent military material in his way, but give me the bedouin....

UNIFORMS AND MEDALS

Mr. Muhamad Ali Ajlouni, the Defence Minister, said in Amman on 26th May 1956, that it had been decided to abolish the shemagh, the red-and-white headcloth of the Legion, which, he said, was not practical and was "not a military head-dress". The soldiers will in future wear khaki berets like those worn by Egyptian and Syrian troops. The imagination boggles at the thought of the bedouin in those hideous and unromantic pancakes.

Mr. Ajlouni is certainly mistaken when he says that the shemagh is not a military head-dress. Look at the tomb of a crusader, or at a coat of arms, and you will see the shemagh in the mantling of the helmets. During operations or on training the soldiers wore it inside out and at a range of a hundred yards or so it merged into the background.

The present regime in Jordan welcomes change for its own sake, and in twenty years time little will be remembered of the uniforms we knew.

The uniform of the Desert Patrol has been described by Glubb Pasha himself. It "was cut in the same manner as their ordinary dress, long robes reaching almost to the ground and long white sleeves, but the outer garment was khaki in colour. With a red sash, a red revolver lanyard, and belt and bandolier full of ammunition, and a silver dagger in the belt, the effect was impressive. Soon the tribesmen were complaining that the prettiest girls would accept none but our soldiers for their lovers."[19] In addition they had magnificent scarlet mantles lined with sheepskin. The head-cloth was kept in position by a twisted headrope of black hair. The soldiers wives worked the borders of their shemaghs into an elaborate fringe known as a "fantasia"; mine were done my the wife of Corporal Saoud Eid. These masterpieces were popular among the bedouin, but the haderi, if their officers were easy going, often left them plain, allegedly to avoid expense. The shemagh was worn by all ranks and arms of the Service, except the police infantry. The police cavalry had yellow ones and the National Guard khaki.

The silver cap badge of the Arab Legion is the same for soldiers and police, but the National Guard have a different badge in yellow metal.

There is a forage cap, the sedara, which may be worn by officers. It is dark blue with a red crown and piping, and gives very little protection, besides being made of poor cloth.

Mr. Ajlouni says that the present black belts and silver buttons will also have to be replaced, for, according to him, they denote a police force and have caused confusion! Service dress, with silver buttons, and with cuffs and pockets of a different cut to British uniform, was issued to all ranks down to and including waqil. Black shoes were worn. The remainder always wear battle dress, which in summer is made of khaki drill and throughout the year is buttoned to the throat. Only waqils and above wear ties.

---

[19] *The Story of the Arab Legion*, p. 103.

Non-commissioned officers wear stripes of the British style, but the metal stars and crowns of officers and senior N.C.O.s are of Arabic design. Cadets wear white gorget patches while they are at the Cadet School, but when they leave they wear silver bars on their shoulders. A cadet has to serve in a regiment for three years before being promoted second-lieutenant — always supposing he passes his promotion exam.

Regiments and formation headquarters all have distinctive lanyards and cloth signs, which latter are worn on the epaulette straps or on the upper arm, and all ranks wear a silver numeral with the words "Al Jeish al Arabi" on their epaulettes. Marksmen wear crossed rifles on the left cuff, and signallers and musicians wear crossed flags or a lyre on the right arm above the elbow.

The other ranks of the police infantry, who wear spiked helmets, have a khaki drill battle dress in the summer and a blue serge service dress in the winter. The police cavalry wear khaki service dress all the year round, drill in summer and serge in winter. There is a red-coated troop of Household Cavalry, who ride grey horses, and carry aluminium lances. Their appearance would be improved if they wore white breeches instead of navy blue. There are still a few Circassians, dressed like Cossacks, who formed a special bodyguard for King Abdulla.

The military police wear white equipment, and regimental police have blue armbands with red lettering on the left sleeve.

All units used khaki bianco, except 7 Regiment and Glubb Pasha's bodyguard platoon, originally drawn from it, who blackened their equipment, presumably with boot polish.

Some officers had blue patrols in winter and a white drill evening dress for summer, but these were not compulsory.

British officers sometimes wore their British patrols, but otherwise they always dressed in Arab Legion uniform.

There are three bands, the red, the blue and the green. In winter they wear khaki battle-dress, and in the summer white service dress. They can be told one from the other by the colour of their lanyards, epaulettes and pipes. These bands are called by the bedouin "The Gipsies of the Jeish"!

The Dead Sea Fleet wore a blue uniform with a white belt, more like marines than sailors.

By 1955 the Royal Jordanian Air Force was wearing sky blue, and had adopted a service dress cap in place of the sedara.

The Gallantry Medal, a plain green ribbon, with a bronze medal bearing a portrait of King Abdulla, is more highly prized than any other. Not very many have been issued.

Medals were issued for the Second World War, and for the Palestine campaign of 1948. Another medal was given for the Iraq and Syria campaigns of 1941, this latter being comparatively rare. There is a Long Service Medal, which other ranks get for fifteen years' service and officers for twenty.

There are in addition three orders: Al Kawkab al Orduniyye, the Star of Jordan; Al Nahda, the Renaissance; and Al Istiqlal, the Independence. The last two are divided into five classes, the fifth being reserved for other ranks, fourth for junior officers and so on.

Many Jordanian soldiers wear British campaign medals earned during the Second World War, while a very few have French medals, won with the Armée de l'Extérieure in Syria. The Cedar of Lebanon is sometimes seen, and the red ribbon of the medal of the Greek Orthodox Patriarch, commemorating the fifteen hundredth anniversary of the foundation of the Greek Church in Jerusalem is not uncommon.

Name: Al Fariq, Rank in the Arab Legion: Lieutenant-General, Courtesy Title: Pasha

Name: Amir al Lewa, Rank in the Arab Legion: Major-General, Courtesy Title: Pasha

Name: Zaim, Rank in the Arab Legion: Brigadier, Courtesy Title: Bey

Name: Qaimakam, Rank in the Arab Legion: Colonel, Courtesy Title: Bey

Name: Qaid, Rank in the Arab Legion: Lieutenant-Colonel, Courtesy Title: Bey

Name: Waqil Qaid, Rank in the Arab Legion: Major, Courtesy Title: Bey

Name: Rais, Rank in the Arab Legion: Captain, Courtesy Title: Bey

Name: Mulazim Awal, Rank in the Arab Legion: Lieutenant, Courtesy Title: Effendi

Name: Mulazim Thani, Rank in the Arab Legion: Second Lieutenant, Courtesy Title: Effendi

Name: Morasha, Rank in the Arab Legion: Cadet, Courtesy Title: Effendi

Name: Waqil, Rank in the Arab Legion: Warrant Officer, Courtesy Title: Effendi

Name: Naqib, Rank in the Arab Legion: Colour Sergeant, Courtesy Title: Effendi

Name: Naib, Rank in the Arab Legion: Sergeant

Name: Areef, Rank in the Arab Legion: Corporal

Name: Jundi Awal, Rank in the Arab Legion: Lance-Corporal

Name: Jundi Thani, Rank in the Arab Legion: Private

A NOTE ON THE TRIBES

The original Desert Patrol was formed to put an end to raiding, and operated initially among the Huwaitat, who live around Ma'an in the South of Jordan. "The Howeytat nation inhabit all the wilderness country above the Sinai Peninsula betwixt the two seas and deep inland: they come down in the Teha'ma border, by the Red Sea, to Wejh."[20]

Under their great leader, Auda Abu Tayi, who loved fighting, the Huwaitat had been allies of Lawrence, and had helped him to capture Aqaba. Continual raiding had weakened and impoverished them, but they were grand military material, responding well to discipline, yet retaining some of their wildness. They are on the whole rather simple souls, full of talk and straightforward in their dealings. There were many of them in 9 Regiment, and they were good soldiers: Ingheimish Hamdan and Rizig Suleiman were typical of the tribe. When the Arab Legion was operating in the desert around Palmyra in 1941, some of the tribesmen, including Za'al Ibu Mutlaq who had fought with Lawrence, hired two trucks and came up to join them! They arrived chanting a war-song. It was a charming gesture, and it seems churlish to add that they had neglected to bring any rations with them.

The Beni Sakhr are the largest of the Jordan tribes, and send many men to the Legion. They are still nomadic, but they have long engaged in agriculture, and for that reason are comparatively wealthy. Charles Doughty, whose *Travels in*

---

[20] Doughty, p. 234.

Arabia Deserta was first published in 1888, has a typical passage about them.

> Bedouins in these highlands are the Beny So'khr, a strong tribe and lately formidable, having many horsemen; so that none durst pass these downs, unless by night time or riding in strong companies. Their intolerable Beduin insolence was checked by a military expedition under the same Mohammed Said now pasha-guardian of the pilgrimage, a valiant and victorious captain, exercised in this manner of civil warfare from his youth. The Aarab easily discouraged, whose most strength is ever in their tongues, and none leading them, were broken, and the Pasha mulcted them of horses and cattle. The B. So'khr being thus submitted to the Dowla,[21] promised for themselves to plough the land as the fellahin. Those tribesmen are now the principal Beduin Haj[22] carriers, from the north down even to Mecca; they are dispraised by their nomad neighbours. Aarab of the borders, there is in them a double corruption, of the settled land and the wilderness: other Beduins speak of them a word in hatred, which is not be believed to the letter. "Wellah (by God) the Sokhur will cut the throat of a guest in the tent." To violate the guest, "the guest of Ullah", in the religion of the desert, is the great offence.

Glubb Pasha, whose book was printed in 1948, says that the principal sheikhs of the Beni Sakhr had taken to agriculture twenty or thirty years previously, but the process evidently began earlier. Their estates lie near Amman, and they are familiar with the city, and at least one, Mithgal Pasha, has his town house and sits in the Parliament. The sheikhs are well-dressed, perfumed and courtly. The Beni Sakhr have reached

---

[21] The (Ottoman) Government.
[22] Pilgrimage.

the transitional stage, between the desert and the sown, and are beginning to lose the primitive virtues. Yet some of them are still very typical bedouins: old Hammad Faleh, known as "Abuna" (our Father) for his grey hairs, was in no way like the settled fellahin. He lives at Muwagger in the desert East of Amman. Still, in general the Beni Sakhr do not make such good soldiers as the Iraqi bedouin, or even the Huwaitat. Perhaps civilization and soldiering do not really go hand in hand.

The Beni Khaled, a small tribe whose "capital" is the village of Hausha near the Syrian border North West of Mafraq, are very like the Beni Sakhr. They have houses and tents, and are only semi-nomadic. There were not many of them in 9 Regiment, and none of them of great note.

In the lava belt in the North of Jordan and in the Jebel Druze in Syria live the People of the Mountain, the Ahl Al Jebel, who are still completely nomadic, having few camels, but many sheep and goats. In the winter they live in the lava belt, but in the heat of summer they prefer the hills. There were many of them in 9 Regiment, mostly rather small in stature, but good soldiers. They paint their eyes to improve their eyesight as they say, but really out of vanity; and they love fine raiment, for at home they were ragged and poor, fortunate if they had dirty sheepskin cloaks to wear. In the Jeish they quickly lose their long matted locks, and are transformed, as if by the magic of their uniforms, into alert and hardy soldiers.

The bedouin from the Wadi Sirhan were well represented; they numbered about thirty, including some of the best officers and platoon commanders; Khalaf Ghassib, Khleif Awwad, Addad Msayeh, Abdallah Dahil, and Warwir Hishal. They are generally considered to be rather slow and thick witted, but, if unlikely to attain high rank, they are a stout-hearted lot. Khalaf, who had the reputation of being one of the bravest men in the Legion, rose to be a company commander, and proved a good one. Khleif did too well on his Vickers machine-gun course and became an instructor at the Arab Legion Training Centre.

To the East of the Beni Sakhr live the Ruwallah, who, except for two good officers who came to us in 1954, were not very strongly represented in the Regiment. One was Second-Lieutenant Nazzal Hleyil, a stout handsome bedouin, who had won the Gallantry Medal in 1948 when he was a corporal. He had been severely wounded in the chest leading his section in the attack on the Sheikh Jarrah Quarter of Jerusalem, and had later been in the 1st Armoured Car Regiment. The other, Second Lieutenant Mseifer Murki, was lean and active, and came to us with a 17-pounder platoon, which was transferred to us from the 4th Regiment of the Artillery. As a sergeant he had led his platoon through a minefield in the assault on Radar in 1948. When he came to us he took the precaution of bringing all his best men with him.

Between the Wadi es Sirhan in Jordan and the Euphrates the Syrian Desert is chiefly inhabited by the Aneizeh, a numerous tribe or confederation of clans, which is also strong in the Nejd. From the latter division of the tribe came Cadet Mteir Dhahi, who had also taken part in the capture of Radar, as a corporal. He was the second man to get inside the Israeli wire — the first was killed. He rose to be R.S.M. of 1 Regiment, and was transferred to 9 on leaving the Cadet School, proving an excellent reliable officer, and a strict disciplinarian.

The Shammar of Iraq and the Nejd were very strong in the Arab Legion. They had opposed Ibn Saud, and, being defeated, were driven Eastwards. These loyal supporters of Glubb Pasha, who had followed him from Iraq, gave many officers and sergeants to 9 Regiment.

Harb, Billi, and Beni Atieh from the Red Sea coast also had little contingents, the latter including my driver Juma'a Faraj whose tribe, in Doughty's day, used to prey upon the Haj caravan. A number of the Harb had been settled in Jordan, and particularly in Zerqa, for about twenty-five years. Their sons, now of military age, are no longer bedouin, but have become typical townsmen, and none the better for it.

The Beersheba bedouin, refugees from Israel, have latterly been enlisted into the Legion and it remains to be seen whether this experiment will be a success. In appearance they are generally rather short and round faced. Not many of them have yet become N.C.O.s and it is difficult to say whether they will become good soldiers. For my part I consider that the more nomadic bedouin, and the ones who live farthest from the centres of civilization, make the best soldiers.

We had few of the Mutair, who are from the central part of Saudi Arabia, but these included Saoud Rashdan.

BIBLIOGRAPHY

The following works have been consulted during the writing of this book:

Miss Winifred Coate: *The Condition of Arab Refugees in Jordan.* Reprinted from *International Affairs.* Vol. XXIX. No. 4. October, 1953.

H. R. P. Dickson: *The Arab of the Desert.*

C. M. Doughty: *Travels in Arabia Deserta.*

Brigadier J. B. Glubb; C.M.G., D.S.O., O.B.E., M.C.: *The Story of the Arab Legion.*

Nelson Glueck: *The River Jordan.*

G. Lankester Harding: *Jerash.* 1948.

G. Lankester Harding: *Petra.* 1938.

H.M.S.O., 1921: Palestine. Disturbances in May 1921.

C. N. Johns: *Guide to the Citadel of Jerusalem.* Government of Palestine Department of Antiquities. Jerusalem. 1944.

Henry Kendall: *Jerusalem City Plan.* 1948.

Stewart Perowne, O.B.E.: *The One Remains.*

Steven Runciman: *A History of the Crusades.*

Sidney Toy: *A History of Fortification.*

Colonel A. P. Wavell, C.M.G., M.C.: *The Palestine Campaigns.*

G. E. Wright and F. V. Filson: *The Westminster Historical Atlas to the Bible.*

ACKNOWLEDGEMENTS

I am greatly indebted to the following who have helped me in various ways in the writing of this book:

J. Adair, Esq.; Major R. Bryant, M.B.E., D.C.M.; Lt.-Col. Pat Gray, and Brigadier A. E. Green, D.S.O., O.B.E.

A NOTE TO THE READER

If you have enjoyed this book enough to leave a review on **Amazon** and **Goodreads**, then we would be truly grateful.

Sapere Books

Sapere Books is an exciting new publisher of brilliant fiction and popular history.

To find out more about our latest releases and our monthly bargain books visit our website: **saperebooks.com**